searching for agabus

searching for agabus

embracing authenticity and finding your way to you

Michael Walrond

BROADLEAF BOOKS
MINNEAPOLIS

SEARCHING FOR AGABUS
Embracing Authenticity and Finding Your Way to You

Cover design: Dan Pitts

Print ISBN: 978-1-5064-8529-4
eBook ISBN: 978-1-5064-8530-0
Printed in Canada

Contents

Deep Longings for Freedom

The only way to deal with an unfree world is to become so absolutely free that your very existence is an act of rebellion.
—Albert Camus

To be beautiful means to be yourself. You don't need to be accepted by others. You need to accept yourself.
—Thich Nhat Hanh

If only it were easy to just be yourself, but in an age of conformity being yourself is a courageous act. I wish it wasn't the case. Living authentically should be the norm. Being true to yourself should be the standard by which we live. Sadly, it is not. Conforming to what others believe we should be is the easy way out, especially when there is reluctance to struggle to be at ease in one's own skin. I am amazed at how many would rather toil to live up to externally imposed expectations than toil to live an authentic life. Neither is easy, but the former leads to a crisis of identity, while the latter leads to self-discovery.

The courageous are fueled by a deep desire to live in the fullness of authenticity. The courageous live boldly and freely in a realm fashioned by their imagination—an imagination that can be stifled and suffocated in an effort to conform to what and whom others believe we should be.

Being courageous in an age of conformity is difficult. It is hard work. This is why many would rather suspend imagination in order to find a resting place in spaces carved out by those who are too fearful and too uninspired to live authentically themselves. This is tragic. Imagine having to lessen yourself so that others feel comfortable. Imagine having to dumb yourself down to standards of acceptability that have been created by those who resist living in the realm of unlimited possibilities. It is sad when we restrain our ambitions so that we can fit into prescribed definitions of who and what we should be.

The awkwardness of our age—an age of mixed signals and confounding voices—is that on one hand, we are encouraged to be the best version of ourselves, and on the other hand, we are expected to conform and fall in line with what everyone else is doing. We are cautioned not be followers, but then we are chastised for wanting to march to our own drumbeat.

Those who do not conform—who do not give in to fear—are called rebels, radicals, or maladjusted by those who do not live lives shaped by their imagination. They insult the courageous to hide their own fear of being courageous.

Tragically, those fearful to live an authentic life have become the standard-bearers for living. They have become the ones we have exalted while minimizing ourselves.

Everywhere we look, from media to social media to television commercials, we are being bombarded with messages that we need to be everything other than who we truly are in order to be seen, admired, valued. Look like this. Act like this. Dress like this. All so that we can be liked—not loved, but liked. We contort ourselves physically, emotionally, and psychologically so that we can be validated and affirmed, unaware that we are slowly losing our freedom to be authentically ourselves. How easy it is to slip into the land of the unfree and become blind to our imprisonment.

The unfree long to be free, but that assumption may only hold true when the unfree know they are bound. That might seem strange. How would the unfree not know they are unfree? But this is what happens when the unfree are so attached to their captivity that they have lost the ability to discern what bondage even looks like. The unfree normalize their bondage to the extent that they no longer recognize the nature and depth of their captivity. What keeps the unfree bound are the blinding bindings on the unfree that make captivity alluring, beautiful, sweet.

Many years ago, in my youth, when I first read the words attributed to Harriet Tubman, "I freed a thousand slaves. I could have freed a thousand more if only they knew they were slaves," I cringed at the thought of someone not being aware that they were a slave. I could not imagine someone being so content with their captivity that the possibility of escape feels offensive. But now, many decades later, I better understand the work of enslavement. It strangles aspirations, suffocates possibility, destroys identity, shatters dreams, and convinces you there is no world beyond enslavement. And when enslavement has done its work, the unfree are not aware that they are unfree.

In spite of the inability of the unfree to fully see the nature of their captivity, I believe that somewhere deep within, in places untouched and untainted by their captivity, the unfree long to be free. Somewhere deep within there are unspoken desires for an unbound life. In fact, we all harbor deep longings for freedom to be our authentic selves. We long to sing a song of freedom. There are lyrics that languish within the unfathomable corridors of the imagination, lyrics that our souls long to release. Deep within all of us, there is music shaped by the rhythms of our lives. And that music and those lyrics often remain hidden, unknown and untouched. Some call it soul music. It is the music and songs of freedom— the freedom to be your authentic self. It is the music whose harmonies make us whole. That music can only be played and the songs can only be sung if you are willing to accept yourself, embrace yourself, love yourself. You must be willing to bask in the glow, glory and grandeur of your authenticity. You must be at ease in the magnitude of your uniqueness. Freedom feels like and looks like *you*!

Imagine the *you* who no longer needs to pretend to be what you are not. Imagine the *you* who refuses to suffer from a crisis of identity because others tell you who and what you should be. That *you* is the free you, the liberated you, the rebellious you, the authentic you.

AUTHENTICITY SACRIFICED ON
THE ALTAR OF INSECURITY

Albert Camus was right when he penned these poignant and powerful words: "The only way to deal with an unfree world is to become so absolutely free that your very existence is an act of rebellion."

That act of rebellion cannot be commenced when the lie that we are not enough is accepted. Rather than self-acceptance, we seek approval from people, spaces, or places that make us feel like we are enough, that validate our worthiness for us. Wanting to be affirmed is not inherently bad, but when it requires us to forfeit our authenticity, it leads to the slow rupturing of the self and the shattering of identity. When we constantly want to be liked, validated, and affirmed, we place ourselves in the hands of those we seek to be validated by. We can become so driven by the addiction to affirmation that we will seek to be validated at any cost. And that drive is instigated by insecurity. Addiction to affirmation sacrifices the true self for acceptance. You lose the ability to see how unique you are. You slowly lose your freedom. You become unfree.

Those desperately wanting validation, addicted to affirmation, will sacrifice sanity, well-being, and identity on the altar of insecurity in order to be liked—again, not *loved*. The need for affirmation can become so intense that you find yourself on a seemingly perpetual mission to prove yourself.

Like those Harriet Tubman encountered who did not "know" they were enslaved, who couldn't imagine freedom, many today are not aware that they are unfree. I used to be one of those persons. I was unfree because it is easier to order my life by artificial standards, determined by others, in hopes that somehow I would be affirmed. I do not speak now as one who has fully arrived at the place of total freedom, but I have broken the chains and begun the journey of self-discovery.

How long are you willing to live with veiled ambitions, carrying dreams deeply hidden in your heart? How long will you continue to lose yourself in order to gain acceptance? How long will you continue to invest energy seeking to prove yourself to unproven people? How long will you mourn about being rejected by people, spaces, or places that cannot handle the enormity of *you* and your gifts?

Rebel. Be brave. The courage that lies deep within you is crying out for you to pursue freedom and live authentically. This is your season to harness the power of your God-given imagination and live the life that you were created to live. You cannot just speak of being free. You must tenaciously pursue freedom, because seeing the possibilities and never walking in them is misery. Let your imagination be the architect of an unbound reality that you construct. It may seem risky and challenging, but you will not be alone. Agabus will be with you. You may not know who he is right now or what he represents, but continue to read this book and you just might find that Agabus is a worthy traveling companion who can help you find an alternative way of showing up in the world.

My friend, the world is waiting for the real you to show up. I believe this with all of my heart.

I did not write this book with the hope of outlining and detailing a particular path to freedom. What follows is no quick and easy prescription There will be no three steps to this or ten steps to that. The journey to freedom, the route to authenticity, is never an easy one, and there is no one way. I trust you to find your own path to what makes you whole. I believe that we each know what our individual path is, we're just afraid of walking alone. I pray that what you read will awaken the courage and bravery you require to rebel against conformity and the need to be liked, and empower you to give voice to the deep longings within you that strike the chord of freedom, of the authentic *you*.

I wrote this book to raise awareness about a particular type of enslavement—what I call addiction to affirmation. That addiction can be broken, authenticity can be attained, but it will require you to come from beneath the shadows of insecurity and self-doubt and be who you truly are.

In *Crime and Punishment*, Fyodor Dostoevsky put it best: "Taking a new step, uttering a new word, is what people fear most."

Therefore, be strong, be courageous, and turn the page.

Future Memories

Death is not the greatest loss in life. The greatest loss is what dies inside of us while we live.

—Norman Cousins

We have two lives, and the second begins when we realize we only have one.

—Confucius

The tears were streaming down my face as the casket was being lowered into the ground. My hero, my grandfather, was gone and there was something painfully final about this moment that was incomprehensible to my fifteen-year-old mind. The pain was excruciating.

It was the first time I had lost someone so close to me. And I was not prepared for shadowy valleys. When you are young, you have a tendency to believe that the people you love deeply, and who love you back, will live forever. You hold on to that hope primarily because you cannot imagine living life without their presence and their love. And up to that point in my life I could not fathom living life without my grandfather's presence, without his love. I believed that he would be present for all the milestones in my life: high school and college graduation, marriage, and the birth of my children. But all of that ended in August of 1986.

I remember the day, just nine months earlier, when I found out that my grandfather was dying. It was December 1985. I was in the ninth grade, and I had just gotten home from school. We lived in an apartment building that was right across the street from the police station in Freeport, New York. It was supposed to be the suburbs, but where I lived was no suburban utopia. My aunt and her family lived in the same apartment building, and on the same floor. My aunt's apartment was close to the elevator and I would have to walk past her apartment to get to mine. On that particular day, as I got off of the elevator, I noticed that her apartment door was cracked open. That seemed strange, especially since it was the middle of the afternoon, and no one was usually home around that time. As I stood in front of the door, I was convinced that someone had broken into her apartment. Trust me, in my neighborhood, living across the street from the police station did not guarantee protection from crime. So I mustered all the courage I could and opened the door expecting to encounter some unknown intruder. Instead, I walked in on a scene that has been etched in my memory.

My grandmother and aunt were sitting at the kitchen table and it was apparent that they both had been crying.

I asked my grandmother what was wrong. She replied, "Junie, it's not good."

"What's not good, Grangran?"

"Your grandfather is dying. He has liver cancer and the doctors believe he only has a month to live."

Her response drastically changed my fourteen-year-old life. I was speechless. How could this be? Nothing about what she said made any sense. How was this possible? The suddenness of it was too much. Cancer? How did he get it? Where did it come from? I was just with Grandaddy the night before and everything seemed fine. I knew he had been complaining about feeling pain on his side, but there was nothing about his complaining that even remotely made me think that death was on the horizon.

I left my aunt's apartment immediately. I felt like running but I didn't. Even at fourteen, I was sensitive to what I perceived as being too dramatic. I walked down the hall to my apartment. For some reason, I did not want them to see me crying. I don't know why, but the tears that I was about to shed felt different. The pain felt different and I wanted privacy. I walked into my apartment, dropped my book bag, took off my coat, and went to the bathroom. I stared in the mirror and began to cry uncontrollably. My tears were winning. My hero was going to die. *My hero was going to die.* I was not prepared, in any way, for that moment. Navigating life as a teenager was hard enough. Death's entrance was making it more difficult. Death had not entered yet, but death hovering over life's possibilities can be more difficult to deal with than the reality of death. The idea of dying is what terrifies us. The idea of no longer being present, missing out, is what we fear. At fourteen, having to deal with death's shadow seemed unbearable.

I was standing outside my aunt's apartment door on that day, believing that an intruder had entered her house. An intruder did enter: death's shadow. Up to that point in my life, based on what I had gleaned from bits and pieces of sermons and Sunday school classes, death was an intruder upon life, an enemy that needed to be conquered. I was led to believe only God could defeat death. After all, God was omnipotent. He, because I had been taught that God was a male (it is interesting how we believe God is a spirit, but patriarchy makes God a gender-specific spirit), was in control of everything. If God is all-powerful and in control of everything, then God should be able to heal my grandfather and beat back death. I stood in the bathroom, looking in the mirror with tears streaming down my face, and I decided to have a conversation with God. Well, not so much a conversation as much as an interrogation, and I had one question for the omnipotent God that my grandfather trusted in: "God, why are you letting my grandfather die?"

Given the way I had come to understand God, it seemed like a reasonable question. I've since come to realize that in moments of crisis, when we find ourselves questioning or crying out to God, it's not for God's answer, but to lament, to declare and name the pain, give voice to the agony. As I questioned God, I was not only giving voice to pain, but acknowledging my confusion about why God seemed disinterested in whether my grandfather—who trusted in God—died, or worse, that God was impotent in the face of Grandaddy's impending death. It was a profound moment in my life. As I look back on that moment, it was the beginning of my anger and resentment that I would harbor toward God for a long time.

I now know that my anger wasn't really with God. The problem was how I was taught to think about God. God wasn't the problem. My assumptions about God were, but at fourteen I couldn't distinguish between my assumptions about God, and God.

My grandfather lived eight months longer than the doctors expected. He was a warrior with an indomitable life force. He was the embodiment of strength and grace. He left me with lessons about living and dying and facing death, lessons that I have never forgotten. He courageously embraced his death the way he had courageously embraced his life and it was clear to me that death did not and could not destroy him. My grandfather meant the world to me. He was my best friend, my confidant, and my biggest cheerleader. There was nothing he wouldn't do for me and in turn there was nothing I wouldn't do for him. He was and is the greatest human being I have ever met and I count it a true blessing to have been loved by him.

On that sweltering day in August of 1986, as they lowered the casket with my grandfather's body into the ground, I stood at the edge of the grave crying profusely. I was inconsolable. An emptiness came over me, a deep brooding. Pain and agony were having their way with me. I was overwhelmed by a sense of helplessness and aloneness. My hero was no more and I would have to face the rest of my life without the physical presence of the man whose love made me whole. I was broken by his death.

My uncle, my grandmother's brother, stood beside me at the foot of the grave. He put his arm around me. Instantly, I thought that he must have sensed, seen, and even felt the depth of pain I was in and sought to console me, but what he said did not ease the pain at all. As we both looked down into the casket's final resting place, he said, with his high-pitched Bajan accent, "Well boy, that's all of our fate." And in an instant, I went from mourning my grandfather's death to mourning my own inevitable ending. My mourning for Grandaddy was interrupted by my mourning for myself. I am sure that my uncle had no ill intent, but his words sounded like a death sentence, and just like that the intruder had broken in and crept into my conscience. I had never really contemplated my own death. Even though I had witnessed my grandfather slowly deteriorate over eight months, the thought that I too would one day die had never really crossed my mind. My uncle's words forced me to confront my mortality. I was abruptly confronted with a jarring reality: We are all future memories.

My grandfather was the embodiment of love and grace. He came from very humble beginnings in Barbados. When he died, he was not a wealthy man. He was a chef and, in my opinion, a culinary master. He had spent some time as a cook on tobacco farms in Connecticut in the '60s. He had also been a chef at some hotels, but for all of my life he had been a chef at a hospital on Long Island. He never achieved fame and celebrity, but understood the peaceful splendor of living and loving. Family was paramount for him. Giving love was no chore for him. His generosity with his love was the overflow that emanated from a deeply rooted and unspoken yearning to live a life that honored the depth and expansiveness of his humanity.

My grandfather's funeral was standing room only. I had never seen so many people in our small United Methodist Church, not even on Easter Sunday. The sanctuary was filled with family, friends, and neighbors. Doctors, nurses, and staff who worked at the hospital with my grandfather lined the walls of the sanctuary. I was amazed at how many people were crying. I had no idea that my grandfather meant so much to so many people. It was obvious from the crowd, the emotions, and the words that were shared about my grandfather that he impacted many people. I felt like my grandfather was some sort of celebrity.

After the funeral, before we made our way to the cemetery, one of his coworkers at the hospital who worked with him in the kitchen shared a story with me about my grandfather. I did not know the gentleman, but I could see that he had been crying. He told me that there was a woman who was a patient in the hospital who was dying from cancer, and that my grandfather insisted on personally delivering her meals to her during his shift. There were others whose job it was to deliver meals, but for some reason he insisted on doing it himself. He did it up until the time that he was no longer able to work because of his own fight with cancer. He must've felt some kinship with her as they were both battling, some unspoken bond that warriors share. His battle brought out the best of him. That was my grandfather.

Throughout the ages, many philosophers and psychologists alike have posited that human beings are the only creatures who are conscious of their impending death, and it is that awareness of unavoidable death that wreaks havoc on the psyche. None of us knows when it will happen or how it will happen, but death is inescapable. We will, eventually, only be spoken of in the past tense. A day will come when people will gather and share fond, and sometimes not-so-fond, memories of our living, and the thought of that can be crushing. It is a truth that we try to hold at bay until the truth breaks through the illusionary barriers that we have created to keep us at a safe distance from our mortality. We arrive and then we depart. That is a brutal truth for those who have dreams of immortality. We are all future memories.

So why do I begin this book with death? I begin with death because death is demanding. It demands our attention in ways that life does not. I wish it was the reverse, but it is death's reminder of the brevity of life that not only forces us to face our finiteness, but encourages us to cherish our days and prioritize our possibilities.

We have been in the midst of a global pandemic since 2020. Coronavirus is a part of common conversation. At the onset of the deadly virus, stories of people overtaken by it and dying alone in their homes left us horror-struck. In New York City, refrigerated U-Haul vans filled with dead bodies because funeral homes had no more room felt apocalyptic. The prospect of death by an invisible enemy was mortifying and caused many of us to evaluate what was really important in life.

I've stood at the bedside of the dying. Awkward moments of silence punctuate the intensity of transitioning. Conversations with the dying are beautifully human experiences and those conversations can be filled with unintended wisdom. In the conversations I have had with the dying, in over twenty-five years of being a pastor, I cannot recall anyone wishing they had more money or more fame. I cannot recall anyone wishing they had a bigger house, more designer clothes or cars. And I definitely never heard anyone in recent times wish they had more followers on social media as they were dying. I have heard those who were dying wish they had more time and more breath to live and to love. More time with family and more time to see the world and more time to create beautiful memories and more time to see the ocean and more time to appreciate trees and more time to value more time. What is of importance to the dying ought to be priorities for the living.

We are all future memories. Life is too short to get lost in the dizzying desire for attention. Life is too short to worry what people think about you. Life is too short to spend time and valuable energy making other people happy while you remain miserable. And life is certainly too short to spend it trying to achieve some sort of celebrity status. My grandfather was not a famous man and the world did not know who he was, but in his sixty-three years of life he lived, he loved, and he served. He lived a deeply authentic, meaningful, and impactful life.

Human acts of kindness, like my grandfather's, that are consecrated with love, do not make headlines. Sensationalism, in all of its forms, on all media platforms, is preferred over substance. Fixation on the superficial seemingly rules. And we are gripped by celebrity culture. Sadly, compromising one's integrity for the sake of being validated in public spaces by strangers is not cringe-worthy. And it should be.

Like my grandfather, countless people live beautiful, anonymous, and authentic lives, unintentionally and intentionally living life beneath the radar. They do not seek ways to be seen. It is enough knowing that they are seen by God. It is enough knowing that they see themselves. Fame is not their goal. They are not attention-seekers. This does not mean that attention may not come their way, especially given the nature of the particular life assignments they honor, but in no way, shape, or form is that a driving force in their lives. They represent an alternative way of being and living in a culture obsessed with self-admiration. A way that will be discovered on our search for Agabus.

Agabus was a real person. He is not a well-known biblical figure. In fact, if I were to ask the average Christian if they have ever heard of Agabus, I am pretty sure the response would be no. There are no writings that have been attributed to Agabus. The two brief accounts in the Bible about him can be found in the New Testament book of Acts. Although he is only mentioned twice in the New Testament, both times he is given the designation as a prophet. That cannot be overlooked. God's prophets shared what God wanted people to know. And Agabus has something to share. As we encounter Agabus, we just might find a way out of our cultural addiction to affirmation and discover the courage to authentically be ourselves and fill the voids created by insecurity.

A Famine in the Land

At that time prophets came down from Jerusalem to Antioch.
One of them named Agabus stood up and predicted by the
Spirit that there would be a severe famine over all the world.
—Acts 11:27-28

I was my hungriest when I hungered for myself.
—Negal de la Casa

In the tenth chapter of Acts something unforeseen happens. The expansion of the Jesus movement continued, but now it would become more inclusive. The early Jesus movement was primarily a Jewish movement. Jesus was a Jewish carpenter, who lived during a time when Jews were an oppressed people under the Roman Empire. His reach was primarily to other Jews. His first followers were Jewish, so some believed that "The Way" — as the movement was known before the use of the term "Christianity" — was an exclusively Jewish movement. One needed to be Jewish. Non-Jewish people could be benefactors of the power of God made known in and through Jesus, but some in the early Jesus movement believed that to be a part of it, one had to be Jewish. That belief would begin to unravel when Peter, who had been in Jesus's inner circle and had become a leader of the early movement, had an experience that changed him and his assumptions.

One day, Peter went up on a roof to pray. While praying he became hungry and wanted something to eat. While waiting for the food to be prepared, Peter fell into a trance. While in the trance he saw the heavens open up and something that looked like a sheet was being lowered by its four corners. In the sheet were all sorts of animals. He heard a voice instructing him to kill the animals and eat. Peter was baffled because according to Jewish tradition, strict rules dictated what could and could not be eaten. Peter refused to kill and eat any of the creatures that were profane or unclean. Then he heard the voice say, "What God has made clean, you must not call profane." This happened three times while Peter was in the trance and then the sheet was taken back up toward the heavens.

Peter was utterly confused by his vision, and while pondering the vision, he heard the Spirit speak to him. He was told that there would be men looking for him, sent by a Roman soldier named Cornelius. When they found him, Peter was to go with them.

The day before Peter had his vision, Cornelius also had a vision. In Cornelius's vision, he was instructed to send men to find Peter and bring him back to where Cornelius resided. Cornelius sent three men who found Peter. They shared Cornelius's vision and believed that it was an angel who gave Cornelius the instructions, and assured Peter that although Cornelius was a Gentile, not a Jew, he was well spoken of by many Jews.

The next day Peter went with the men to meet Cornelius. Peter said to Cornelius and all who were assembled at Cornelius's house, "You yourselves know that it is unlawful for a Jew to associate with or to visit a Gentile; but God has shown me that I should not call anyone profane or unclean." God can change God's mind. Peter began to preach. He preached about God. He preached about what God had done and was doing through the carpenter. He preached about the kingdom of God. He preached the good news.

While Peter was preaching, to his amazement, the Holy Spirit fell upon all the Gentiles—non-Jews—who heard, and they began to praise God. Peter then ordered those who traveled with him to baptize the Gentiles. Gentiles, who had been viewed as profane and unclean, were now ranked among the believers.

News about Gentile believers spread. Other leaders of the Jesus movement questioned Peter: "Why did you go to uncircumcised men and eat with them?" Peter had violated Jewish laws, customs, and rituals. But Peter passionately shared with them how, upon hearing his preaching, the Gentiles became filled with the Holy Spirit and began to praise God, exactly as had been the case with Jews who followed The Way.

Still, some Jewish adherents to The Way were skeptical about Gentile conversions and refused to preach to them, but that did not stop the inclusive expansion of the Jesus movement. Gentiles were not only being brought into the movement by Jewish believers, but by other Gentiles. Although some Jewish believers were not pleased with this, many were excited and rejoiced. Followers of The Way were still being persecuted, and the expansion of the movement must have felt like a burst of new life for the fledgling movement.

A FAMINE OF AUTHENTICITY

The expansion of the movement could really be felt in Antioch. It was in Antioch that the believers were first called Christians. Acts tells us that prophets from Jerusalem, the Jewish religious center, came down to Antioch. One of them named Agabus, led by the Holy Spirit, predicted that there would be a severe famine all over the world. And with that prophecy, Agabus enters the biblical narrative.

Biblical prophets were not popular people. They were viewed by many as messengers of misery, disseminators of gloom and doom. The prophet's identity was synonymous with the prophet's proclamation. What they had to say was more important than who they were, which is why we are not given much background material about them. The writers of the stories about the prophets made it clear that the message the prophets delivered had little to do with the prophets and everything to do with God. Prophets were God's messengers. Their words of warning could be piercing. Their declarations could be damaging. Their descriptions of the consequences of disobedience could be terrifying. They held mirrors up to nations and individuals, forcing them to see themselves in ways that their arrogance or shortsightedness did not allow them to see. Prophets may have found favor with God, but were not well liked by the people.

When Agabus journeys from Jerusalem, he is not alone. Other prophets travel with him, but Agabus is the only one named. No background information about him is provided. We know nothing about him. He is a prophet, which means that what he says is of divine origin.

What Agabus has to say is not strange. Famines were not foreign to the people of his day, so it is not what he says that is telling. It is when he says it.

Agabus arrives to Antioch just as the Jesus movement was expanding, and although the inclusivity was not welcomed by all, it still signaled that the teachings of and about Jesus were transcendent. The gospel was for all. The gospel did not conform to social or cultural constructs designed to divide. What was happening in Antioch was a hopeful sign that the gospel of the carpenter could truly reach the world. Agabus's words of warning arrive in the midst of this hopeful time: A severe famine was coming.

Famine is a scarcity of food marked by disease, starvation, and death. A famine is caused by natural disasters as well as underlying social and political factors. Scholar and activist Duncan McLaren once said, "Famine is not caused by a shortage of food; it is caused by a shortage of justice." Most famines are created by human beings.

When Agabus asserts that a severe period of hunger is approaching, he may not be merely speaking about a food crisis. Perhaps he was simultaneously asserting that there were social and political forces at work undermining life. Agabus is admonishing the believers in Antioch to be aware that while the movement is expanding, tough times were ahead. A famine was coming. When Agabus arrived in Antioch his prophetic warning to those who were part of the fledgling Jesus movement was a reminder that although growth and progress were happening, they ought not become so blinded by the growth that they do not prepare for a time of famine ahead. In the midst of a time of prosperity, a crisis was ensuing.

After hearing Agabus's prophecy, the leaders of the Jesus movement came together, gathered resources, and sent relief to believers in anticipation of the oncoming famine. They heeded the warning and made adjustments to lessen the impact of the famine.

Agabus's words of warning are just as timely now, but with one difference. The famine is not coming, the famine is here. It is not a famine of food. There is a deep hunger for authenticity—a hunger for persons who are unwilling to trade their authenticity for approval. But this famine is not surprising given the times we are in. To be sure, we are living in a time of constant technological advancement—advancement that takes place at a breathtaking speed. These advancements have increased human potential, possibilities, and power to literally transform the world for the good, and the growth and expansion of social media is one of the manifestations of these advancements. But social media has also contributed greatly to fostering a cultural climate in which the constant need for public and immediate validation has produced consequences just as great as the advancements.

We live in a tragically shallow age marked by over-sharing and self-absorption, and social media has become the sanctuary for the superficial. Disingenuous flamboyance is applauded while the beauty of living in one's truth is scoffed at. Hollow relationships are normalized and we are constantly distracted by a dangerous, dysfunctional, and overinflated sense of self-importance.

Selfishness and greed gnaw at the margins of our culture. Reckless egos are intoxicated by the aroma of their opulence. Fraudulent personalities seek to cripple and undermine the meaning of authenticity, while rabid insecurities are masked by false bravado and pretentiousness.

The self-obsessed, self-engrossed, and self-centered are celebrated while irresponsible consumption and materialism are paraded as the signs of success. And there is seemingly no limit to how far people will go to garner attention in order to have their self-esteem bolstered by those who may have no interest in their well-being.

A passing glance at the current cultural moment shows that a hunger for authenticity exists because there is a deeply unsatisfied hunger for attention and almost all of us have felt the cravings. The hunger for attention is a hunger to be seen, to be validated, to be valued. This hunger is real and growing, but I believe that the hunger for authenticity is greater.

The wounded soul of our culture is groaning for people to be audaciously authentic. Brené Brown reminds us that "authenticity is the daily practice of letting go of who we think we're supposed to be and embracing who we are." The key to authenticity, according to Brown, is embracing who we are, but what if that is the problem? What if embracing who we are is difficult because we don't see anything worthy of embracing? And instead of embracing that which we deem unworthy, we make the decision to embrace a version of ourselves that can garner the approval of others. When that decision is made, freedom is lost and we drift farther and farther away from who we really are.

We can never really be free if we are not authentically ourselves.

You may be thinking, *How can I authentically be myself if I never knew who I really was? How can I find my way back to myself when I did not know who I was in the first place?* But you do know who you are, and reclaiming that clarity means confronting the forces at work that created the constant need for affirmation and approval. Let me introduce you to Joseph.

The Road to Authenticity

Stop acting small. You are the universe in ecstatic motion.

—Rumi

Our deepest fear is not that we are inadequate. Our deepest fear is that we are powerful beyond measure. It is our light, not our darkness that most frightens us. We ask ourselves, who am I to be brilliant, gorgeous, talented, fabulous? Actually, who are you *not* to be? You are a child of God. Your playing small does not serve the world.

—Marianne Williamson

About twelve years ago, I met Joseph. A mutual friend of ours reached out to me and asked if it was OK to give one of his friends my number. He told me that his friend Joseph was going through a rough time and thought he could benefit from a conversation with me. I agreed and Joseph called about an hour later. I had no idea that Joseph and I would talk on the phone for nearly three hours.

Joseph shared that he felt lost. Joseph was extremely accomplished and successful, but at the time of our conversation it became clear that none of that meant anything to him. He revealed to me that, as a child, he had experienced physical abuse at the hands of his father. Joseph recounted several episodes of abuse and talked about the scars on his body that were still evidence of his father's rage. Joseph felt there was no rhyme or reason to the abuse. Joseph was a straight A student, but on occasions when he would get a B on a test or a quiz, he would be beaten. If his clothes weren't folded properly, he would get a beating. If Joseph was watching television and the TV was too loud, his father would beat him. As Joseph recounted the numerous episodes, I heard the pain and trembling in his voice as he told me of not just physical abuse, but also verbal and emotional abuse. His father's words made Joseph feel worthless and shunned. He continually put him down and at times publicly degraded Joseph in front of his friends. Although Joseph was forty years old when we spoke, I heard the voice of a hurt young boy in every sentence he spoke. His father never celebrated him. Joseph couldn't recall a time when he ever heard his father tell him how proud he was of him. He had no memory of his father ever saying that he loved him. Joseph was a wounded man.

I asked Joseph about his mother. Silence, but I could hear him sniffling. He was crying again. His mother died when he was ten. She had a massive stroke when she was forty. I thought to myself that this bit of information was the key to understanding his father's behavior. Maybe his father was mourning and grieving his wife. He could not emotionally handle the loss, so he took out his pain on Joseph. Joseph quickly crushed my assumption when he told me that his father's abusive ways started well before his mother's death.

His tears over his mother's death quickly turned to a tone of anger. "She never stopped him. She never stopped him. She never protected me. She left me alone. She left me alone." Joseph harbored anger toward his mother for not protecting him from his father and felt her death was a form of abandonment. Joseph was a wounded man.

I asked Joseph what kind of relationship he had with his father at the time of our conversation. "We talk, but he hasn't changed," he said. "I graduated from college, got my MBA. I have accomplished more than I ever could've imagined and not one time has he ever told me that he was proud of me or that he loved me. Nothing I do is ever enough for him."

I asked Joseph if he was married. He told me that he had been engaged twice to different women, but both times he was the one who ended the engagement and the relationship. He went on to say that he had given up on the idea of marriage, that he was fine not ever having a serious relationship but enjoyed the several "not-so-serious" relationships he had with various women.

Toward the end of our conversation, I offered Joseph very little advice. It wasn't that I had no opinion about why Joseph felt lost, but after years of pastoral care and counseling I learned that sometimes the two greatest gifts you can offer are your presence and a listening ear. That is what I offered Joseph instead of my opinions. I prayed with him and recommended he consider seeing a therapist. Joseph had no idea that a couple of months before our conversation I had begun therapy and it had been a godsend for me.

I never heard from him again until about four years ago, when to my surprise, Joseph showed up at the church one Sunday and stayed after the end of service to talk with me. He introduced himself as the man from that one conversation eight years prior, because we had never actually met, and I asked him how he was doing. He said life was amazing. He was married and he was the happiest he had ever been. He told me that a year after our conversation he had mustered the courage to take my advice and began seeing a therapist and that therapy had changed his life. He then asked if I had some time to talk later that week. When we talked, our conversation was much shorter. He shared with me some of the things he discovered about himself during his years of therapy.

He talked about the long-term impact of the physical and emotional abuse he had suffered as a child. He spoke with clarity and I heard a tone of healing in his voice. He acknowledged that when we talked years before he felt his world was unraveling. He felt empty. He felt a void in his life and couldn't explain it. Through therapy he realized that he had lived with feelings of unworthiness because of the abuse. He constantly heard his father's voice and words in his head that made him feel he was never enough. He excelled professionally, in part because he always felt he had something to prove. He was moving from accomplishment to accomplishment, always trying to gain approval from his father that never came. In fact, Joseph came to understand the futility of wanting something from someone who is incapable of giving you what you need. He sought approval in every aspect of his life to feel valued. With all his accomplishments and success, he became unrecognizable to himself because he had lost the capacity for self-approval. He had lost a sense of who he was.

Therapy also helped him understand why his relationships with women were challenging. Losing his mother was traumatizing and he was also bitter because he felt she didn't protect him from his father's abuse. He didn't trust women and, subconsciously, he was afraid of being abandoned by women. Thus, he would pre-emptively end or sabotage the relationship before he could be abandoned and hurt. He tended to end relationships when he felt let down or unprotected. Joseph also realized he was drawn to difficult, borderline abusive relationships because they were in his comfort zone, what he was accustomed to. He hoped to receive approval from people who, like his father, couldn't or wouldn't validate him.

The Joseph I spoke with four years later was on a path of healing because he realized that he was not the problem. And with that realization he began to honor the best of who he was. Joseph had to not only identify the sources of his anguish, but he also had to do the work of loving himself and valuing himself. This was at the heart of his journey of self-discovery and healing. It was through therapy that Joseph was able to connect to who he was before the abuse started, and he discovered the beauty that existed before he was engulfed by pain. He reconnected with who he was before the seemingly never-ending quest for validation cloaked his identity.

THE AGABUS AWARENESS

Many of us are like the Joseph I spoke with twelve years ago—losing ourselves by seeking approval that can never satisfy our deep wounds. Agabus represents a particular kind of awareness that can begin the healing journey. The writer of Acts does not give us any background information on the prophet Agabus other than his name, but that is something. His name has a meaning. Agabus means "the father's feast or joy." In other contexts, it means "God's feast or joy." When I discovered the meaning of Agabus's name I was immediately moved. A feast is a large meal at which something is celebrated. Joy is a feeling of great pleasure and happiness. I never thought about what God's feast could be or would be, but the idea that God could provide a feast resonated with me. God's feast is God's provision during hungry times. For those who know deep sorrow and sadness the joy of God resurrects hope. My mind began to race and immediately went to this thought: *I am God's feast and joy.* The thought of it was powerful, empowering, liberating. Not only I, but we are God's feast, we are God's joy. You are God's feast. You are God's joy. You are Agabus!

In our current hungry times, there is a craving for authenticity. These are times when we yearn for people who can be boldly true to who they really are. Agabus represents the awareness that we are God's provision, God's reason for celebration and God's pleasure and happiness. In doing so, we become "God's feast" in the midst of a famine. When you live *your* life, as your authentic self, you become just what this hungry world needs. You become God's feast. You become Agabus. The search for Agabus is the search for your true self. That is a journey of self-discovery.

Only you can take the journey of self-discovery and find your way back to who you really are. No one can do that work for you.

For me, God is the source of all, the ground of all being. God is that spirit and energy that brings all things into existence. Just imagine for a moment that you and I are God's reason for celebration, that you and I are what brings God pleasure and happiness. We are not flawless. We are not perfect. We make mistakes. We have faults. We have shortcomings. We are not always at our best. We do and say things that we are not proud of. But none of that takes away from the fact that we are God's feast, that we are God's joy, that we are Agabus. At times, sorrow and suffering can enter our lives and hope can even seem fleeting, but none of that negates who we are. We are God's feast. We are God's joy. We can be so consumed with being so many things for so many people in order to gain some validation, that we forget to just "be."

I wonder what my life would have been like if I grew up with the awareness that I was God's feast or joy. I wonder how that knowledge might have impacted Joseph in those days when he felt lost and confused about who he was. The knowledge of who we are in God's eyes can not only bolster our self-esteem but can also be that which beats back self-doubt and the enormous power our insecurities can have over us. The awareness of being God's joy and feast is no quick fix or cure for those who are addicted to affirmation. You will not suddenly be healed by this awareness, but it can be the thing that helps you begin to love and embrace yourself. This awareness can be the starting point from which you begin to live your authentic life. If you mean that much to God, then you can begin to mean that much to yourself, and when you mean that much to yourself, you no longer spend your time seeking to gain approval from others.

Earlier I said that we are in the midst of a famine—there is a hunger, a craving, for authenticity. These times hunger for people who can boldly be true to who they really are. God has provided a feast in this famine. Until now I never thought about what God's feast could be or would be, but the idea that God could provide a feast resonates with me. For those who know hunger, those who are in a famine, God's feast is God's provision during hungry times. *You* are God's feast. You are God's provision during these hungry times. And here's the key: When you live *your* life, as your authentic self, you become just what this hungry world needs.

The world is waiting for you. Learning to live in your authenticity is not an easy journey. No one can take the journey for you. No one can do that work for you. But I know you can find your way back to you. After all, you are Agabus!

The Birth of Insecurity

Most people are other people, their thoughts are someone
else's opinion, their lives a mimicry, their passion a quotation.
—Oscar Wilde

You have been criticizing yourself for years, and it hasn't
worked. Try approving of yourself and see what happens.
—Louise L. Hay

The horrors of the child, left unchecked and unresolved,
become the unshakeable insecurities of the adult. I know this
well. For while I say and believe that I am God's joy, that I am
Agabus, and lean on the knowledge that I am God's joy, for
much of my adult life I have wrestled with insecurities. Fear
has been the architect, but anxiety has the laid the foundation
upon which my emotional frame was built. I was ten years old
when I felt the darkening of noonday. Everything happened so
fast. It was early October of 1981. I was in my grandmother's

bedroom sitting on the edge of her bed. As a child, I loved being in my grandparents' presence. I always felt a sense of safety when I was in their bedroom. My grandmother noticed a small lump on my face. She asked me if I had noticed it before. At ten, I was not in the business of scrutinizing and analyzing how I looked. Sadly, that would not last for long. The lump was on the right side of my face next to what is known as the parotid gland. She touched the lump and thought it felt a little unusual. She informed my father and told him that she was concerned about the mysterious lump on my face, and within a week I found myself in the office of my pediatrician with my mother.

Initially, my pediatrician didn't quite know what to make of the mysterious lump on the side of my face. It wasn't really noticeable. When my head was turned to the left, the small lump would stick out and become more visible. The pediatrician referred us to an ear, nose, and throat surgeon and that is when things started to intensify. What just seemed like a small lump to my family and me took on new meaning for the doctors. Terms that neither my parents nor I had ever heard were now becoming part of my ten-year-old vocabulary. Words like tumor, malignant, benign, and parotid gland became words that I repeated without full understanding, but from the reactions of the adults around me, nothing about these words felt or sounded good. In fact, the words that I heard and the reactions I sensed were subtly birthing an anxiety that nestled in my spirit and lingered within me for years to come.

Several weeks of doctor visits followed. I was poked and prodded more than I can remember. I had so much blood drawn in such a short period of time that I once asked my mother if I could ever run out of blood. She assured me that I would not run out, but she could not assure me that the needles would not hurt. I was never afraid of needles; I had no reason to be afraid before then, but by that point they were the enemy and I was afraid. It's amazing how the uncomfortable repetition of painful moments creates fear. It was a lot for a ten-year-old to process. It felt like a never-ending process.

After weeks of testing and meeting with different specialists, my parents and the doctors came to a decision: I would have surgery. I had a tumor growing on my parotid gland and the surgeons weren't going to just remove the tumor— they were going to remove the gland as well. It would be a very delicate surgery because the gland was located near the nerves in my face and if something went wrong in the process of removing the gland, I could lose feeling on that side of my face.

As the date of the surgery approached, I gained a deeper sense of the seriousness of the situation. It was the Sunday before the surgery and my family and I were attending church. It is safe to say that I was a church boy—at least that's what my friends who lived on my block called me. My family was very religious and we attended church every Sunday. I can't say that I enjoyed going to church, but I did not have much say in the matter, much like I had no say regarding the surgery. On that particular Sunday, I remember straining to stay awake. Sleep seemed to always show up on my pew and befriend me, and every Sunday our relationship blossomed. Suddenly, I heard the pastor say my name as he invited my family and me up to the front of the church for a special prayer.

My family surrounded me as the pastor instructed them to all lay their hands on me. All of my family that attended service that morning formed a circle around me. I felt hands on my head, my arms, my shoulders, and my hand and I could feel my grandmother's unmistakable hand on the side of my face where the lump was. My head was down and my eyes were closed. I didn't quite know what to make of the moment. The pastor said many words during that prayer, most of which I have since forgotten, but certain words have remained since that day. Words like surgery, grace, mercy, healing, healer, protection, and love still remain with me. I raised my head and opened my eyes during the prayer only to see that everyone was crying. My father was crying. I never saw him cry before. His tears scared me. I cried and I questioned. Why did the pastor really call us up to the front? Why is everyone crying? Why is my father crying? What is the surgery really about? Will it hurt? I did not raise any questions about my own death. It would be five years before those questions would be the spawn of death's shadow.

During the car ride home from church the silence rang loud. I had not really been afraid of the word *surgery* until that Sunday. No one in my family ever cried about my surgery until that Sunday. I now found myself wishing that Sunday would never end because the next day was the surgery. When we arrived home, I asked my mother if I was going to be alright. She reassured me that I would be fine, but the trembling in her voice and the tears at the church had betrayed her. She was trying to reassure herself that her little boy, her firstborn, would be alright. To this day I cannot imagine what she must have felt. At the time of my surgery, she was three months pregnant with my brother. She was pregnant with possibility, yet grieving the pain of what had been born. Her little boy, her firstborn, was having surgery.

The morning of my surgery, I remember driving to the hospital with my parents. Several times my father asked me how I was feeling, and every time he asked, I would nod my head and tell him that I was OK. But I wasn't OK. I was terrified. Since church the day before, I was overwhelmed with fear and dread. I remember that my biggest concern, as it would be for most children undergoing such a procedure, was whether the surgery would hurt. I didn't really understand the explanation the surgeon gave me for anesthesia, but he told me that I was going to go to sleep and when I woke up everything would be over. I had only one question: "Will it hurt?" He assured me that I would not feel a thing during surgery. He was right. I felt nothing during the surgery, but the pain I would feel after the surgery and for decades to come would seem insurmountable.

I woke up in the recovery room feeling groggy and completely disoriented. The surgery took a few hours. My throat was sore and my face and head were bandaged. I was scared again. I began to cry and called out for my father. He was the one who had taken me to most of my appointments prior to the surgery. He had been with me through every-thing, so I called for him because I wanted to feel safe again. The nurses allowed him to enter the recovery room and his presence was calming. The discomfort was still present, my throat was still hurting, but I felt better because I was not alone.

My family lined the walls of the hallway outside of my room as the nurses returned me after recovery. My grand-mother and my mother were crying and appeared very upset as I was rolled past them on the way to the room. I did not understand what the cause of it all was. But apparently, after my surgery was finished they never changed my gown. They brought me back to my room with blood stains on my gown. The sight of the bandages and the blood-covered gown was too much for my mother and grandmother. That was the sort of thing my father would have noticed back in recovery, and he would have demanded that the nurses put a new gown on me before my family saw me. I honestly believe that in that moment he was more focused on his little boy—his firstborn—not the gown. He held my hand all the way from recovery back to my room. That was his focus. Needless to say, my father had them change my gown.

Shortly after returning to the room the surgeons came by to check on me. They explained to my family that the surgery went well and that there were no issues or complica-tions. They told me that I was amazing. I took their word for it—after all, I was asleep and had no memory of my amazing performance. The doctors informed my parents that they were still waiting for the pathology report. At the time, I had no idea what that meant. But the doctors were waiting on the pathology report of the tumor to find out whether it was malignant or benign, whether it was cancerous or not. The report came back a few days later indicating that the tumor was benign. I'm sure that was a relief for my family. But my horror would begin the first night in the hospital.

After the doctors left, my family began to disperse and go home. My aunts and uncles left, my grandparents eventually left, and it was just me and my parents in the room. I would feel some pain, but the medication they were giving me guaranteed that the pain would come to pass and not come to stay. I was glad about that. My biggest concern through the entire ordeal was whether I would be in pain, and the pain medication I was receiving intravenously guaranteed that my pain would be at a minimum. But I quickly discovered that there was some pain that no medicine would be able to prevent.

I remember my mother continually looking at her watch and I soon found out why. Visiting hours were coming to an end and my parents would have to leave. It was 1981 and hospital policy was different and strict back then. No one could stay with me. My parents tried to break the news to me as gently as they could but nothing could stop my tears. I cried profusely, begging them not to leave, but there was nothing they could do. The hospital policy was the hospital policy. My parents left and I was alone with my tears. I cried and I cried. I was devastated. The nurses came to my room and tried to comfort me; they tried their best, but they were not my parents and none of them was my mother.

I finally cried myself to sleep, only to be awakened in the middle of the night by the touch of a nurse with needle in hand. Blood had to be drawn and my bandages had to be changed. And that was my cycle of horror for two weeks. It was traumatizing. It was terrifying. I was ten years old and everything was absolutely unbearable. The daytime was not that bad. There was a daily rotation of family and friends, and when they had to leave their departure did not wreak havoc on me. But every night, when my parents would leave, I would be devastated. I cried myself to sleep every night only to be awakened almost every night for more needles and a change of bandages.

My room had a glass window and I could see people walking back and forth in the hallway. On numerous occasions there would be visitors coming to see other patients, and as they walked by my room, I could hear some of things they would say as they looked through my window: *I wonder what happened to him? Did he have brain surgery? That's so sad. Does he have cancer? Was he in a car accident?* These were just some of the things I would overhear. It got to the point where I would lie in the bed with my back to the window and my head under the sheets because I didn't want anyone to see me. My hurt and I were hiding. The crying never stopped, and as the days passed I became angrier and meaner. I was mean to the nurses and very uncooperative. I remember at some point one of the nurses complained to my mother and she fussed at me a little, but my behavior didn't change. I was in deep pain, and at ten years of age I had no way to fully process it. It is hard for children to process grief, pain, suffering, and despair. They know fun, sadness, laughter, and tears. I was sad and there were many tears.

During the two-week stay in the hospital, my physical pain eventually subsided but the emotional damage had just begun. I couldn't sleep at night, I hated being alone, I became afraid of the dark, I hated doctors and hospitals, and I became terrified of needles—but that was not the worst of it. The day before I was discharged, the doctor removed the heavy bandages from my head and face and put on smaller ones, but not before giving me a mirror to see my face. As he gave me the mirror, he told me that the swelling had gone down considerably and for a moment I was relieved; that is, until I looked at myself in the mirror. There was a large incision on my face that extended from the top of my ear to underneath my chin, my face was extremely swollen and, worst of all, I was unrecognizable to myself. The boy in the mirror scared me. I didn't forget the person I saw in the mirror that day because that was the face I kept seeing for the next thirty years of my life.

I was released from the hospital around Thanksgiving but there was nothing in my mind to be thankful for. The happy, fun-loving child that I was before my traumatic experience was quickly fading. My smiles felt forced, the tears flowed more often, and I felt an unshakeable sadness that, for the sake of survival, I learned how to camouflage at a very young age. As I got older, I mastered the skill. The wound on my face eventually healed, but thanks to my keloid skin, the scar grew bigger and more and more visible. With that came horrible teasing and rejection by my peers. Children can behave cruelly at times, and in my case the cruelty was brutal. I was bitter and angry. I hated mirrors. I hated what I saw when I looked at them because I always saw that wounded, swollen face. I couldn't see anything else. But strangely, I couldn't *stop* looking at mirrors either. I couldn't walk past a mirror without pausing to take a glance, hoping that I would look different but it was to no avail. I always saw that little boy with the wounded, swollen face. I was so damaged that all I could see when I looked at myself was damage. Notice I did not say I saw "the" damage. I saw damage. My wounds—physical, emotional, and psychological—became synonymous with who I was. I was not a damaged child; I was damage. And worse, I believed that everyone saw me the same way I saw myself. I never felt like I was enough.

I tell the story of my ten-year-old self because all of our insecurities have an origin story. And like Joseph in the previous story, those origin stories often take place in our childhood. My insecurities were birthed over two weeks in a room in a hospital on Long Island, New York. It would be wonderful if I were able to outgrow the pain and despair I experienced. I wish that my insecurities faded the older I got and the more I matured. I really wish that were the case. But for me, the truth is that I lived most of my life in that hospital room. I went to college in that room. I became a father in that room. I became a husband in that room. I even became a pastor in that room. That room was my dwelling place for a long time.

When were your insecurities born? For they have a birth date that is not the same as your birthing. No child comes into this world with insecurities. Life happens, trauma happens, pain happens. Noondays are darkened and suddenly the child feels as though they are no longer enough. Our insecurities mark the places where the bleeding began and the wounds became visible. Tragically, the pain does not always push us closer to ourselves; it pushes us away from ourselves. We seek to avoid the painful spaces and places, and when we feel that we are that painful space and place, self-avoidance is the form of escape we choose. How many journeys have you taken in an effort to get away from yourself? How many times have you tried to find yourself in someone else only to lose them *and* yourself? How many times have you created multiple identities because of the level of discontent you felt about yourself? How many times have you created myths about yourself in order to be seen, known, and heard?

Our insecurities are the driving force behind our desire for attention. They are the initiators and instigators of our hunger for affirmation and validation. And once you have been seized by your insecurities and they have taken control of your life, no matter how beautiful that life appears, you will not be free. But then again, maybe you do not mind being unfree, because I am fully aware of the beautiful prisons your insecurities can build. And when you allow yourself to be seduced by those beautiful prisons, your freedom goes on life support. And the only path to redemption is to realize that being disliked is the price you may have to pay for your freedom. And that freedom is the environment that is necessary to fully embrace that you are enough, that you are God's joy, that you are Agabus.

The Beauty of Anonymity

While we were staying there for several days, a prophet named Agabus came down from Judea. He came to us and took Paul's belt, bound his own feet and hands with it, and said, "Thus says the Holy Spirit, 'This is the way the Jews in Jerusalem will bind the man who owns this belt and will hand him over to the Gentiles.'" When we heard this, we and the people there urged him not to go up to Jerusalem. Then Paul answered, "What are you doing, weeping and breaking my heart? For I am ready not only to be bound but even to die in Jerusalem for the name of the Lord Jesus." Since he would not be persuaded, we remained silent except to say, "The Lord's will be done."

Acts 21:10–14

The obscure outlast the obvious.

—Lao Tzu

For Paul, returning to Jerusalem was personal. From the time he was sent out from Antioch to preach, teach, and further the expansion of the Jesus movement, his gaze was on Jerusalem.

He traveled to many places with a burning desire to preach to those who were open to hearing the good news. Because of the expanded inclusivity of the movement, wherever Paul went he was usually met with two reactions: There were those who received him and those who vehemently rejected him.

In Antioch, there were some who were jealous of Paul and they publicly persecuted him. In the city of Iconium, Paul was stoned by some who vehemently opposed him. In Lystra, he met a man who had been unable to use his feet from birth. Paul commanded the man to stand up, and when the man stood up and began to walk, people were so amazed by what Paul had done that they thought him to be one of the "gods." Paul replied that he and his traveling companion Barnabas were not gods, just mere mortals who were charged to preach the good news. And once again, those violently opposed to Paul stoned him and dragged him out of Lystra. Wherever Paul traveled, many lives were changed after hearing him preach and he was also opposed, persecuted, and viewed as an outsider, an agitator, a disruptor.

However, no matter where Paul's journeys took him, something within him deeply yearned to get back to Jerusalem. In his past, he had arrested followers of the carpenter and was now part of the Jesus movement. He had sought to destroy the movement and was now an adherent of it. Jerusalem was the place from which he received his marching orders to persecute the followers of the carpenter. It was in Jerusalem where he imprisoned those he now called friends, family, and co-laborers. He wanted to go back because he was a changed man. Paul wanted to introduce those who knew his past to his present. The persecutor was now the preacher. For Paul, returning to Jerusalem was personal.

While en route to Jerusalem, Paul and his traveling companions encounter the prophet Agabus. This time Agabus's prophecy was not of famine, but of imprisonment. Agabus warns Paul of the impending doom awaiting him in Jerusalem. He does it in dramatic fashion. He takes Paul's belt, binds himself with the belt and he tells Paul that this is what will be done in Jerusalem to the man who owns this belt. The message was clear. The image was familiar to Paul. Agabus tells Paul that he will be bound, held captive, and maybe even killed.

Paul is not moved by the words of the prophet. He has already accepted that he might die and nothing can be said to dissuade him from continuing his work. In fact, after hearing these words from Agabus, Paul is more committed to going to Jerusalem. He makes it clear that he is not afraid. He is not only ready to be bound, he's ready to die, if need be, for the cause of the carpenter. It's a heroic moment for Paul. It's a moment of passion and commitment. Paul understands that going to Jerusalem may cost him his life, but he is undeterred. He was going to Jerusalem.

INDISPENSABLE ANONYMITY

Agabus is a minor background figure in the grand narrative of the Apostle Paul. Most of us have never heard of

Agabus. There have been no books written about Agabus. No tales told about Agabus. Acts records him as a prophet. He is a divine messenger, an almost anonymous prophet. And even though he is only directly mentioned twice in Acts, he is considered a saint in the Catholic Church and the Eastern Orthodox church. These churches, to this day, honor Agabus with a feast day, an annual celebration. Although anonymous to most, his impact was so critical that some religious institutions do not want him to be forgotten. Agabus is an example of those, like my grandfather, who have worked and lived their lives in what is called "indispensable anonymity."

I came across that phrase when reading the obituary of Ruthie Tompson written by Margalit Fox. Every now and again I read the obituary section of the newspaper. I am often intrigued by how a person's life is summed up in paragraphs. Writing obituaries is an overlooked art. It takes great skill to write a narrative summation of a person's life in a way that does not dishonor the dead or minimize their life. One day, I came across Ruthie Tompson's obituary. The words above the obituary captured my attention: *Ruthie Tompson, Invisible Hand Behind Pinocchio's Nose, Dies at 111.* My mind was immediately taken back to when I was a child watching the cartoon movie *Pinocchio.* Fond memories of my youth were called to remembrance, and I felt compelled to read about Ruthie.

Ruthie Tompson was among a number of women who worked for Disney in the 1930s, '40s, and beyond as animators in what Margalit Fox called "indispensable anonymity." These were women who were not known, but whose contributions were critical to the success of Disney Studios. Fox writes that John Canemaker, an Oscar-winning animator and historian of animation, when speaking about Ruthie said, "She made the fantasies come real." Her keen eye for colors and details enabled her to critically analyze the countless drawings that made up an animated movie. She helped "breathe life" into the original animated features like *Pinocchio, Fantasia, Dumbo,* and *Snow White.* Ruthie Tompson lived for 111 years, but the majority of the world did not know and will not know who she was. But for Disney, her gifts, her talents, her abilities, her presence were absolutely necessary.

Ruthie Tompson's indispensable anonymity reminds me of the countless unnamed Black grandmothers and mothers, sisters and daughters, aunts and nieces who remain anonymous, but were the backbone of the Civil Rights Movement. They breathed life into the movement. They were the invisible hands guiding the movement. Their courage, bravery, and tenacity were indispensable. There would be no Civil Rights Movement without their contribution and leadership.

So many critically important and impactful people remain anonymous because we have a tendency to focus on the foreground, not the background. We focus on people visible and obviously seen. And we do not always pay attention to those whose lives have been blurred out in the background. Any movie cinematographer will tell you that the background of any scene is what makes the foreground come alive. Even though the focus is usually on the foreground, the background adds depth and complexity to the scene.

Our tendency to focus on what and who is in the front contributes greatly to the current cultural addiction to attention. Many want to be in the foreground and, tragically, background people and anonymous lives do not always get the attention they deserve. Thus, the need to be in the foreground becomes a deep desire, especially by those who live their lives through the filter of insecurity. Whether we want to admit it or not, we are in the grips of narcissism. Self-centeredness, selfishness, excessive self-admiration, and feelings of entitlement rule the day. We are living in a narcissistic time, at a narcissistic moment, and in a narcissistic culture.

We have always known people whom we considered egomaniacs or pathological narcissists, but what is different about this current moment is the impact of social media on narcissism. Social media has deepened the narcissistic impulse by deepening the desire for fame and celebrity status. Attention must be sought and social media platforms like Facebook, Instagram, Twitter, or TikTok are used to fulfill a need for attention and popularity, and they are addictive. We all want our presence on the planet affirmed, but for some, that means attention must be sought at all costs to garner "our fifteen minutes of fame."

ANONYMITY AS AN ATTEMPT TO FLEE TRAUMA

The opposite of fame is anonymity. History is filled with numerous people who were not famous—nor were they celebrities—but their lives had indispensable value. Some, like Ruthie Tompson or the women of the Civil Rights Movement, were anonymous because of social constructs, cultural attitudes, and patriarchy.

Anonymity can also be a choice. Many choose anonymity every day, driven to anonymity as an antidote to a toxic addiction to attention, to counter losing themselves in a quest for validation and approval. The illusions they have created for the sake of attention become unbearable. The psychic fracturing that can take place is emotionally, physically, mentally, and spiritually crippling. The public criticism that comes from strangers through various social media outlets can be agonizing. In those cases, retreating into anonymity, and canceling social media accounts, is necessary for the maintenance of sanity.

We do not talk as much about the negative impact that behaviors intended to gain recognition and validation have on those who practice them, but far too many have been deeply damaged and wounded seeking to be liked, not loved. The cost of pursuing fame and validation can become so great that anonymity becomes a place of escape, to get away from the attention they have longed for that has now turned against them, not necessarily a place of healing.

ANONYMITY IS BEAUTIFUL

There are those for whom living in anonymity is not an attempt to flee trauma. They are committed to living fully in their authenticity without pursuing attention. Attention may come their way, but it is not their aim, desire, or goal. People like my grandfather, whose impact on so many lives cannot be disputed and yet he lived life under the radar. He was simply and profoundly committed to being the best version of himself every day without seeking accolades or notoriety. He totally embraced who he was. He knew he was enough.

Ralph Waldo Emerson once wrote, "To be yourself in a world that is constantly trying to make you something else is the greatest accomplishment." To be true to yourself in a world that is relentlessly sending messages that you are not enough is a rebellious act. This world will try to beat you into submission and lure you to forfeit your right to define yourself and be at peace with yourself.

Some of the most empowering and transformative moments in my life have come on the heels of learning to draw closer to myself and embrace myself and love myself and appreciate myself and value myself. In those moments, the freedom I felt was radiant; in those moments, I left the ranks of the unfree and drew closer to myself. One of those moments took place many years ago in a conversation I had with my wife.

We were driving back to North Carolina from Florida. We had taken the kids to Disneyland. It was 1999 and our son and daughter were eight and five, respectively. They had an amazing time and it brought my wife and me joy seeing them so happy. It was a nine-hour drive from Orlando, Florida, back to Durham, North Carolina, and my wife and I would alternate driving every two hours so that one of us could sleep while the other was driving. We left Disney at about five that evening after giving the kids one last day at the park. We knew it would be a difficult drive back. We were about five hours into the drive and I was driving. I woke my wife up from her sleep and shared something that had been gnawing at me for a few weeks.

I had been pastoring a small congregation in Durham for about three years at the time and I told her, "I think it's time to move on to another church."

She was a little agitated because I woke her up during her rest period, but she asked, "Why do you feel it's time to leave?"

"The church is too small for me," I said honestly to her. "With my training and degrees, I should have a bigger church." I cringe now as I write this, remembering what I said. I was young—twenty-eight—and a little full of myself. I had gone to Morehouse College and Duke University Divinity School and, in my youthful arrogance, I thought those credentials should have guaranteed a larger assignment. I felt unseen at that small church. I was hearing about the achievements of my peers and colleagues. I was jealous. I wanted to be known, heard, and seen. I felt that could not happen if I remained at the congregation in Durham.

"How do you expect God to give you more when you haven't learned to love what God has already given?"

My wife's response shook me. But her words forced me to look at myself. My insecurities were getting the best of me. I was comparing myself to others instead of being at peace with who I was and where I was. Her words were jarring because as I continued to reflect on what she said, I realized that my issue wasn't the church. I was the issue. It wasn't just the church that I hadn't learned to love. I hadn't fully learned to love and value myself. I was so busy comparing myself to others that I forgot to love what God had already given. God had given me myself.

My wife slept for the rest of the drive home. She didn't drive again. While she and my children slept, I spent the next four hours at the wheel encouraging myself and speaking words of affirmation to myself. I expressed gratitude for that congregation and gratitude for myself. I had never done that before. It was a transformative moment. By no means was I healed from my insecurities during those four hours, but I felt free—free to love *me*. The only thing comparable to the freedom I felt was the indescribable joy I experienced. That joy was hard-earned.

No one ever really knows the things you go through for the sake of wanting to be validated. Attention-seeking is an attractive distraction that attempts to ease the anxiety caused by low self-esteem. The person we become while attention-seeking on our quest for validation and affirmation is an illusion. The quest leads back to self-avoidance.

But the joy you feel in the moments that you embrace yourself is blissful. They are moments of profound awakening when the joy is no longer what you feel but who you are. I remember the first time I said, "I am joy." It was during that drive back to North Carolina. I did not say it with fear and trembling. I said it with boldness, because those words were hard-earned.

As a believer and follower of the teachings of the carpenter, I not only embrace that I am joy, but I also embrace that I am God's joy and so are you. God finds favor in me and you. God accepts me and you because we have been fearfully and wonderfully made in the image of God. Why spend time clamoring for attention from people when we know that we are seen, known, and heard by God? I shared in the previous chapter that one of the meanings of the name Agabus is "God's joy." Think about that for a moment. When I say and believe that I am God's joy, it is another way of saying that I am Agabus. We are Agabus. Knowing that we are God's joy is a way to keep insecurity at bay when we feel we are not enough.

The Danger of Looking for Likes

If the world hates you, be aware that it hated me before it hated you. If you belonged to the world, the world would love you as its own. Because you do not belong to the world, but I have chosen you out of the world—therefore the world hates you.

John 15:18–19

The world will ask you who you are, and if you don't know, the world will tell you.

—Carl Jung

When you are born in a world you don't fit in, it's because you were born to help create a new one.

—Unknown

The words spoken by the carpenter in John 15:18–29 are difficult to hear. They are not words of endearment. These words evoke anxiety. And these are the words he spoke to those who were the closest to him: his disciples. I have often wondered if I could have been a disciple back then. Would I have been able to walk away from the things I held dear in order to grab hold of the unknown? Would I have been able to separate myself from the spaces, places, and people whom I loved and that supported me? I would like to think that I would, hope I would.

The late German theologian Dietrich Bonhoeffer reminds us that when the carpenter calls someone to follow him, it is an invitation to death. The call to discipleship may very well lead to literal death, but it's also a death of old ways of being and belonging in the world. It is a call to renewal, a call to transformation, a call to surrender. Although the challenges that come with discipleship can be intense, there are also moments that are filled with affirmation and encouragement.

There are moments in which you will experience things you have never experienced and feel the presence of God in ways you never could have imagined. The carpenter affirmed those who responded to the call. He encouraged them to live beyond the confines and limitations placed upon them by the oppressive system under which they lived.

The carpenter reassured them that their mistakes do not define them, and that God is like the father of the prodigal son, always waiting to welcome them home with open arms when they have gone astray. The disciples are reminded that—when they fear that they have fallen short and redemption seems impossible—that's when the love of God meets them in the midst of their misgivings and loves them back to wholeness. Those moments of grace were filled with words of encouragement, and they were beautiful.

But then there are the words from the carpenter like the ones found in the fifteenth chapter of the Gospel of John:

If the world hates you, be aware that it hated me before it hated you. If you belonged to the world, the world would love you as its own. Because you do not belong to the world, but I have chosen you out of the world—therefore the world hates you.

This is challenging to hear. The carpenter informs the disciples that the world will hate them because the world hated him. The hate would probably not exist if they belonged to the world, but they do not belong to the world; they have been chosen by the carpenter. What a weight to carry. It is one thing to have people who do not like you, but to be told that the world will hate you is a different kind of emotional burden to bear.

Jesus was not really saying that the entire world would hate them. They were being told that when you make a decision to follow Jesus and honor his teachings, you may be viewed as hostile by forces and mechanism of culture. That somehow, when you make the decision to honor the best of your humanity, you become problematic to those who honor the worst of their humanity.

When you seek to feed the hungry, clothe the naked, give drink to those who are thirsty, visit those who are in prison, and visit those who are sick, you become such a disruptive force that the "world" will hate you. When you speak a word of liberation to those who are oppressed, people will hate you. When you honor the inherent dignity of all human beings, the world will hate you. Jesus did not sugarcoat his words.

I wonder how Jesus's words would be received today, especially when we want to be publicly affirmed and not publicly canceled. We want the approval of strangers, and when you yearn for the superficial approval of people you do not know, it is an indictment of the shallow lens by which you view life. When you spend your days looking for likes and posting for praise on social media, the last thing you want to accept is the idea that the world will hate you.

Whether we like to admit it or not, we all desire the affirmation of others. We seek external validation that makes us feel better about ourselves. The child wants their parents' approval in order to feel valued. The employee seeks a good performance evaluation to verify competency and efficiency. The student desires the teacher's approval and recognition as an indicator of accomplishment and achievement.

The desire for affirmation can be healthy. It serves as a form of motivation and becomes the rationale to strive for excellence. The desire for approval becomes the force that pushes individuals to maximize their potential and move beyond the boundaries of mediocrity. It can be the impetus for greatness and a stimulus for achievement. Still, there is a crippling dark side to the desire to be affirmed. This dark side is unveiled when the desire is not just a contributing factor for one to gain prominence but instead becomes a manifestation of massive insecurities.

It is stifling to live in that fragile space where the approval of others is as important as the air you breathe. It is tragic when the only way you feel some sense of worth is when that worth is confirmed by other people. I know this to be true because I was one of those people who lived with a low estimation of who I was.

My insecurities, born of my childhood trauma, had such a stranglehold on me that I became a person who constantly yearned for validation from others in order to value my own significance. But when you live life that way, pretty soon you find yourself so dependent on the opinions of others that you lose the ability to affirm yourself. I had become so consumed with what people thought about me that I was no longer recognizable to myself.

I was allowing my self-worth to be based on how I was valued by others. That was foolish and depleting. Ultimately, I was forced to look within and engage in a journey of self-discovery. I had to find my way back to myself after having lost myself in other people. My desire for affirmation was based on my insecurities, my insecurities were based on the things I felt I lacked as a person, and the things I felt I lacked as a person were based on peoples' assessment of me. It was a revolving door. And as long as I continued to need the affirmation of others, my insecurities would remain intact—and as long as my insecurities remained intact, I would never feel as though I were enough.

That revolving door is difficult to escape, especially now when it is fashionable through social media to see how many likes you get for the posts you make. It gives instant gratification and an instant sense of approval. But there is danger in looking for likes. Why? Because it does not heal your need for approval, it perpetuates it and intensifies your thirst for it. In fact, you need it so badly that your life and your sanity rest on the hope that people will like you.

There is a way out of the revolving door. It begins by taking ownership of your anxieties. I know that may not be easy, but it is absolutely necessary. What does that mean? Stop looking for other people to heal you. By leaving your potential healing in the hands of those who contribute to your imprisonment only deepens the wounds. You may be wounded, but being wounded does not mean you cannot participate in your own healing. Trust me, your healing will not happen unless you embrace the reality that you can participate in your own healing. Do not place that responsibility on anyone else. You are a wounded healer.

Next, accept a harsh reality: Not everyone is going to like you. Why? Disapproval is normal. It is par for the course. It is part of the journey. And here's what you also need to know: When people do not like you, it may not have anything to do with you. Let me explain.

There is a psychological evaluation known as the Rorschach test, in which people are shown inkblots and their perceptions of the inkblots are used to analyze their frame of mind. The test is not about the inkblot. What one sees in the inkblot is a gateway into what and how the person thinks or feels about themselves. "What do you see?" is usually the question asked when the inkblot is placed in front of an individual. The response gives insight about the individual who's looking at the inkblot.

Here's what I want you to know: You're the inkblot. What people think about you is not really about you. It's a revelation about them. How they feel about you reveals something about them, and why would you use the way others see themselves as the way to evaluate how you see yourself? When you find yourself feeling crippled by the opinions of others, remember that you are the inkblot. Not everyone will like you. More importantly, it is hard for others to like you if they do not like themselves.

Lastly, another way out of the revolving door is to untangle. I was listening to the radio one day and heard a psychologist discussing the negative impacts of social media. I wish I had heard the whole discussion and knew who he was, but he said something that caught my attention. He said that one of the things that must be done to lessen dependency on the affirmation that comes from social media is to untangle one's worth from the likes received on social media platforms. When a person is tangled, it means they have become twisted together into a confused mass.

To be untangled means to be free from a twisted and confused state. Do you want to be free? Do you want to be free from the confusion that comes when you base your self-worth on who likes you or who doesn't? Maybe the key to untangling is knowing and believing that you were born worthy—that you were born with value. You were born with everything you need to be a beautiful expression of humanity. You are strong enough. You are wise enough. You are smart enough. You possess everything you need to be who you are.

The writer Jessica Valenti put it best. She said, "Wanting to be liked is like being a supporting actor in your own life, waiting for cues from the actors, assuming they have the next lines." Looking for likes reduces you to being a supporting actor in your own life. Why? Because you are dependent on other people's thoughts and opinions to determine the trajectory of your life. That is not freedom.

For the sake of freedom, honor that which is genuine within you. Dare to honor the best of yourself. Show up every day in the majesty of your uniqueness, in the glory of your God-given identity. Show up every day as the person God has called you to be. That's your task. That's your charge. Measure your life against your heart—a heart that was created and loved by God. When affirmation comes from within and from God, the heart begins to heal and the insecurities begin to diminish. After all, you are Agabus. You are God's feast. You are God's joy. You are whole, complete, and lacking nothing. Lean into that knowledge and you will realize the futility of looking for likes.

A Reason for Rejoicing

After this the Lord appointed seventy others and sent them on ahead of him in pairs to every town and place where he himself intended to go. He said to them, "The harvest is plentiful, but the laborers are few; therefore, ask the Lord of the harvest to send out laborers into his harvest. Go on your way. See, I am sending you out like lambs into the midst of wolves. Carry no purse, no bag, no sandals; and greet no one on the road. Whatever house you enter, first say, 'Peace to this house!' And if anyone is there who shares in peace, your peace will rest on that person; but if not, it will return to you. Remain in the same house, eating and drinking whatever they provide, for the laborer deserves to be paid. Do not move about from house to house. Whenever you enter a town and its people welcome you, eat what is set before you; cure the sick who are there, and say to them, 'The kingdom of God has come near to you.' But whenever you enter a town and they do not welcome you, go out into its streets and say, 'Even the dust of your town that clings to our feet, we wipe off in protest against you. Yet know this: the kingdom of God has come near.'"

Luke 10:1–11

> The seventy returned with joy, saying "Lord, in your name even the demons submit to us." He said to them, "I watched Satan fall from Heaven like a flash of lightning. See, I have given you authority to tread on snakes and scorpions and over all the power of the enemy, and nothing will hurt you. Nevertheless, do not rejoice at this, that the spirits submit to you, but rejoice that your names are written in Heaven."
>
> Luke 10:17–20

Their anxiety must have felt overwhelming, for the carpenter's words did not ease any fear they must have felt. "I am sending you out like lambs into the midst of wolves." These were the words that the carpenter declared to seventy of his followers who were about to embark on a life-changing journey. The carpenter was sending the seventy, in pairs, to the places he intended to visit. In those places the seventy were to be the embodiment of the kingdom of God. Their presence, wherever they went, was a sign to let the people they would encounter know that God had not forgotten about them, the kingdom of God had arrived. The seventy were to signal that God was doing a new thing. And the new thing God was doing was being done with and through ordinary men and women. They were on a mission—a divinely inspired journey. And Jesus sent them forth with these fear-provoking words, "I am sending you out like lambs into the midst of wolves."

This carpenter did not bolster the confidence of the seventy. He did not ignite their passion, nor did he create a sense of excitement. "I am sending you out like lambs into the midst of wolves." He shattered any illusions they might have had about their journey. Their work would not draw crowds of thousands. They would not receive some privileged status, nor be idolized or adored. They were like lambs; they would be surrounded by wolves. The carpenter wanted them to understand that from the beginning. The imagery was clear. The possibility of being slaughtered was always on the agenda.

If those words weren't chilling enough, he then tells them to make this potentially harrowing journey empty-handed: "Carry no purse, no bag, no sandals; and greet no one on the road." The seventy weren't just lambs, they were empty-handed, defenseless lambs. They were to carry nothing on their journey that could have eased their anxiety or given them a sense of security. And since they were sent out in pairs, they could not even depend on the collective presence of seventy. They were thirty-five pairs of lambs headed into packs of wolves.

The carpenter gives them directives for their journey. Whenever they entered a house or a town they were to enter with words of peace. If that peace was received, they would stay and eat and be provided for by those who welcomed them. In those towns where they were received, they were to cure the sick and let the people know that the kingdom of God had arrived. But whenever they entered a town where they were not received, they were to go into the streets of the town and announce that they were shaking off the town like shaking the dust off their feet. Most importantly, they were to keep moving on to the next town.

With these warnings and directives, the seventy were sent out. Empty-handed lambs, possibly going off to slaughter, taking nothing that would give them a sense of safety and comfort on what would be a perilous journey. Just the thought of that must have felt daunting. They were not being sent out as predators. Jesus gave them no guarantee of success and no assurances that they would be received or accepted. And they themselves were not completely sure what the kingdom of God really was. Without giving them real clarity about the kingdom, the carpenter was clear about how demanding the journey would be. And off they went.

The journey of the seventy is our life journey. At times, life can be confusing and dangerous. We wish that we could journey through life in beauty and bliss, but we live with no such guarantees. In moments of crisis and chaos, we hope the challenges and the obstacles are short-lived, but no one journeys through life unhurt or unscathed. I learned that lesson at ten years old and I have the scars to prove it. There are times when it feels like calamity is a constant companion, sorrow an ever-present sidekick, with shadows constantly hovering. I've also learned that life gives moments of unspeakable joy. In those moments, it feels like you are living wide awake with your dreams and the sun is always shining on your possibilities. Life is truly a journey through the dawn and the dark.

Just as the carpenter tells the seventy that they will experience rejection and acceptance on their journey, we too experience both in life. You will be liked by some and possibly hated by others. There will be spaces and people who like you—wonderful. There will be spaces and people who don't like you—wonderful. Who you are and how you are cannot be based on whether you are or are not affirmed. Some will accept you and others will reject you. You cannot waste your time keeping a tally. Focus on living the life you were created to live and let the chips fall where they may. You cannot be held captive by the whims and opinions and fickleness of people you encounter along the way. The carpenter admonished the seventy to learn this. Agabus learned this as well.

As I shared before, only two places in the Bible name Agabus and they are both in Acts. Another reason why Agabus is revered as a saint in the Catholic and Eastern Orthodox churches is because he was believed to be one of the seventy. The Bible gives the names of the twelve disciples and although many more men and women were numbered among the followers of the carpenter during his lifetime, the twelve men who formed Jesus's inner circle are consistently named. In the Gospel of Luke's account of the seventy, they remain nameless, shrouded in mystery.

Hippolytus of Rome was a priest and theologian of the Christian church who lived during the late second century and early third century. Among his writings is a small one entitled *On the Seventy Apostles of Christ*. In that writing is a list of the seventy disciples/apostles. Although there are doubts about the accuracy and validity of Hippolytus's list, some view it as potentially valid because of the lineage of Hippolytus's teachers. He was a student of Irenaeus, a bishop of the church, who lived from the mid-second century into the third century. Irenaeus was a student of Polycarp, the Bishop of Smyrna, who lived from the mid-first century into the second century. Polycarp was believed to be a disciple of John the Evangelist, who was one of the twelve named disciples. Included in Hippolytus's list was the prophet Agabus.

Other lists of the seventy were created that many believed had more validity. A list was developed by Dorotheus, the Bishop of Tyre, who lived from the mid-third century into the fourth century. He was the teacher of Eusebius, the famed fourth-century historian, who chronicled much of the early history of the Christian church. A list of the seventy compiled by Dimitri of Rostov, a seventeenth-century priest and teacher, was recorded in his writing *The Lives of Saints*. It was Dimitri's list that went on to be accepted by the Orthodox Church. In each of these lists, Agabus was named as one of the seventy.

It is widely accepted by the Catholic Church and the Eastern Orthodox Church that Agabus was among the seventy that were sent out as empty-handed lambs.

When Agabus and his companions returned from their journey, they returned rejoicing. They returned with joy. But I am not convinced that they left with joy. The carpenter's words as they set out must have caused anxiety, trepidation, and downright fear, but those emotions didn't make the return trip. They did not start with joy, but the seventy obeyed the directive given by the carpenter. If they had allowed fear to deter them, they would have missed out on joy. If they had let anxiety stop them, there would have been no reason to rejoice. They honored the assignment. Agabus and his companions moved forward in faith because they trusted the one who sent them. Because the carpenter trusted them, they learned to trust themselves.

Before I share their reason for rejoicing, I want to point out what the seventy *did not* share when they returned. When the seventy returned from the journey, they did not talk about who accepted them or who rejected them. They made no mention of any obstacles they encountered. They returned without giving any account of the places they visited that were the most welcoming or the most hostile. No tally of who liked them versus who hated them. Why didn't they talk about any of that? Maybe Agabus and the disciples learned one critical thing: None of that matters. Who liked them or rejected them did not ultimately matter. They returned giving no mental and emotional energy to those who approved of them during their journey. They didn't get bogged down in the quest for attention and approval that could have depleted and damaged them.

The seventy were rejoicing because of what they discovered about themselves. When the carpenter sent them out, he told them that wherever they were received, they were to preach and heal the sick. They left with the expectation that they would have the capacity to preach and to heal. What they did not expect was that they would also have power over demons. They returned to the carpenter rejoicing, saying, "Lord, in your name even the demons submit to us." There they were, a group of ordinary people, nothing particularly special about them, yet they discovered that they possessed power that made demons tremble and submit. The discovery of their gifts, abilities, and power would have never happened had they allowed fear to cause them to abandon the assignment. They went on the journey and the reward was not just what they were able to do, but what they were able to discover. So, they rejoiced.

Imagine what that kind of joy feels like. It is a joyous feeling when most of your life you believed that there was nothing extraordinary about you, then suddenly you find yourself with the capacity to do the extraordinary. Have you ever blown your own mind? Have you ever surprised yourself? Have you ever celebrated yourself? Many of us have forgotten, or never learned, how to celebrate ourselves. Maybe that's why we so desire to be celebrated and validated by others.

When you know how to celebrate yourself, you don't feel compelled to look for likes or post for praise or spend hours scrolling through social media, becoming depressed because you believe your life does not compare to the amazing images you see posted by others. How many times, after surfing through social media, have you felt unaccomplished, inadequate, or worthless? You felt this way after seeing others "living their best lives." That can happen easily, but when you engage in the comparison game, you are comparing yourself to glimpses and snapshots of someone else's life, and the "Insta-life" you may be envious of may be a total illusion. The technological advancements in social media have had many benefits, but they have also reinforced insecurities and deepened the anxiety that comes with those insecurities.

Celebrate your uniqueness, accomplishments, gifts, power, and identity. It is an unmatched experience. It is an overlooked but necessary form of self-care. When you know how to honor and celebrate yourself, you reduce the likelihood of embarking on misguided journeys to seek out people who will honor you. When you can honor yourself, love yourself, and embrace yourself, you'll experience an exquisite freedom—the freedom to be yourself.

Honor the Assignment

His Lord said unto him, well done, thou good and faithful servant: thou hast been faithful over a few things, I will make you ruler over many things: enter into the joy of the lord.

Matthew 25:23, KJV

Whatever you do, strive to do it so well that no man living and no man dead and no man yet to be born could do it any better

—Dr. Benjamin Elijah Mays

"God, what did I miss? What did I not get? Did I honor the assignment?" These are the questions I hurled in God's direction in anguish upon returning from a forty-day sabbatical that I had no intention of taking. Just six weeks prior to my departure, I clearly heard God's voice tell me to leave for forty days. It was an overwhelming experience, but I knew it was God that I heard and God's timing could not have been worse.

It was October of 2007 and I had been the pastor of First Corinthian Baptist Church (FCBC) for a little over three years. Things were going extremely well. I had been working really hard and the church had been growing and thriving in ways I never could have imagined. So why would God want me to leave at that time? There was much I had planned over the next several weeks. The last thing I wanted to do was to abandon my plans, but I had to go, and I had to leave immediately. After all, I was leaving out of obedience to God.

So I did it. It all happened so fast, there was very little time to think it through. I packed my car and just started driving. It was a little scary. I had no destination mapped out, but I was convinced that everywhere I needed go would be revealed during the journey.

As I traveled, I would often wonder why God wanted me to leave. Was there something that God wanted me to see, to hear, to do? I started believing that, with every destination, with every experience, with every encounter, there was something sacred waiting to be revealed. I started looking for what God wanted me to see, hear, or do. At almost every turn I started asking the same questions: "What is my assignment? God, is this it? Was I supposed to get this? Was I supposed to talk to her? Did I say the right thing to him? Was I really supposed to go there? Should I have stayed there instead? Am I doing the right thing?" Over time, every day seemed to be filled with endless questions and, worst of all, God was not responding to my questions. For forty days, the voice that told me to leave had nothing to say. God was silent.

The day I returned home I felt a deep sense of sadness and the sadness would not leave. Everyone was excited to have me back, but I was not excited to be back. I felt that I missed what I was supposed to see, hear, or do. I was beating myself up. One night, after I had been back for a couple of days, I woke up from my sleep and told my wife that I was going to go to the church. It was two o'clock in the morning. She looked at me strangely, but she had been sensing my anxiety. I got dressed, grabbed a couple of pillows, some blankets and went to the church.

When I arrived at the church I made a small pallet out of the blankets, knelt down, and started talking to God. "What did I miss? What did I not get? Did I honor the assignment?" The voice remained silent and eventually I fell asleep. I woke up later that morning and was getting ready to go to the bathroom when suddenly, God spoke.

"What's wrong?" I responded, "God, did I miss it? What did I not get? Did I honor the assignment? I feel like the forty days was in vain." The voice's reply jarred me. "Who told you that you were supposed to get something?" "What do you mean? You called me away for forty days and I thought there was something you wanted me to see, hear, or do." God's response humbled me: "I was satisfied because the day you left told me that you knew how to be obedient. Your obedience was all that I wanted, and you gave that to me the day you left. The rest of the time was for you to rest and enjoy yourself."

The truth of the matter was that I did miss something. I missed enjoying myself. When I left, I assumed that there was some deep meaning attached to why I was being told to leave. Some sacred secret that God was going to share with me. I had so many assumed and desired outcomes attached to my journey, to my assignment, that I missed the actual assignment. I missed joy. I missed myself. I did not enjoy joy because I couldn't imagine that joy was sacred. I learned a valuable lesson: Sometimes you have to honor the assignment without being attached to particular outcomes.

It can be a tough lesson to learn because there are times when we want to know that the assignment that we are committing to will yield a particular fruit. What if honoring the assignment *is* the fruit? What if obedience is the fruit? In my case, the fruit was my leaving, not what would happen after I left. That means that my feelings of sadness, frustration, and disappointment that weighed me down during and after my forty-day sabbatical, were unnecessary self-inflicted wounds. All the emotions I felt—the hurt, the pain, the tears—were a result of my assumptions and desires, not God's directive. Being attached to the outcomes or results of obedience can actually cause you to miss the joy of the journey.

I wonder what would have happened to Agabus if he had attached particular outcomes to the assignment he was given by God to warn Paul. Agabus was a prophet, a divine messenger, and his assignment was to warn Paul of the trouble awaiting him in Jerusalem. That was it. That was all he was told to do. That was the assignment.

Paul did not heed Agabus's warning. Paul chose to go to Jerusalem. Everything that Agabus said would happen, did happen. But what if Agabus believed that his assignment was also to convince Paul not travel to Jerusalem? What if Agabus determined that his success or failure was based on Paul's response? If that were the case the prophet would have felt as though he failed, that somehow, he had let God down. The assignment would have become an act of ego. Agabus would have been assessing his efficacy as a prophet on the response to his prophecy.

The truth of the matter is that you can obediently honor the assignment given and still be viewed as a failure according to the definition of others. In the Old Testament, Jeremiah was such a prophet. He was not well-liked during his time. He was called by God to warn the people of God that Jerusalem was going to be destroyed as a result of disobedience. The people were worshipping false gods and straying away from God's commandments and laws. Jeremiah did not want the assignment. He did not want to be the prophet of doom and gloom.

In spite of his hesitation and reluctance, he submitted to the call of God, the assignment upon his life. Jeremiah's preaching was difficult for the people to hear or receive. No one paid attention to Jeremiah's preaching. People made fun of him. No one believed him. He was so emotionally wounded by his experiences that the book of Jeremiah frequently depicts scenes of him crying. He was known as the "weeping prophet." Jeremiah preached for forty years and very few believed him or were persuaded by what he had to say. He was constantly rejected, beaten, imprisoned, and eventually killed. Jeremiah was not "successful" according to what one might consider success, but he honored the assignment. And now, no one who reads the Old Testament can avoid Jeremiah. An entire book in the Bible is named after him—an "unsuccessful prophet." Jeremiah's story reminds us that even when we are viewed as unsuccessful, we can still be found to be in favor with God because we honor the assignments given.

The Bible never relates what happened to Agabus after he carried out the assignment he was given by God to warn Paul of the trouble awaiting him in Jerusalem. We know Paul didn't heed the warning, but Agabus's assignment was to warn Paul. Two thousand years later, Agabus is still footnoted for completing the assignment, not for preventing the dramatic outcome of the grand narrative of the Apostle Paul.

We must be careful that we do not attach our egos to the assignments. Once ego is attached to the assignment, we not only lose sight of the assignment, but we personalize everything we do in the name of the assignment, and pretty soon the entire assignment becomes about us. The agenda shifts from the assignment to the outcomes. Once outcomes are the focus, success becomes the fixation. Once being successful becomes a fixation, then measuring and determining indicators of success becomes the critical.

Once you begin looking for ways to measure success, it's almost impossible to avoid engaging in comparison to other perceived models of "success." Once the comparison game begins, feelings of inadequacy are usually the starting point, and that can quickly lead to seeking the approval of others, especially those you view as successful.

Being successful in life is not a problem; neither is the approval of others, but it can be dangerous when we constantly seek validation from others and use that validation as a way to measure success. Honor your life and honor the assignments in your life and do so without a desire to be seen, heard, or known. It is a breath of fresh air to lungs depleted by narcissism to meet people who do not seek attention or accolades. Honoring the assignment means using your gifts, your abilities, and your power for the sake of the assignment itself.

The work of so many today is motivated by their desire to raise the profile and elevate their personal platform—to capture more followers and get more likes. It is dangerous to want followers, but not want to encounter your authentic self. It is dangerous to want likes, but not love yourself.

There is something beautiful about living and honoring your life without being concerned about who sees you. There is beauty in anonymity.

Honor your assignment, bask in the glow of your own uniqueness. Everything you do doesn't have to be posted. Everywhere you go doesn't have to be posted. There's beauty in being. There's beauty in being present. There's beauty in being alive and enjoying amazing moments of life without the pomp.

Now you may be saying to yourself, "Pastor Mike, what you are saying sounds good. I want to honor my assignment, but what is my assignment? What am I to do with my life?" I'm glad you asked. Turn the page.

The Goal of Life

Life, we learn too late, is in the living, the tissue of every day and hour.

—Stephen Leacock

Life is not measured by the number of breaths we take, but by the moments that take our breath away.

—Maya Angelou

As a pastor, I encounter many people who find themselves trying to navigate the complex, perplexing waters of life. Those waters can be treacherous and unyielding. Some succumb to the tumultuous currents of life and accept a role as the target of assault. Viewing oneself as a victim destroys one's sense of power and agency. This defeatist attitude undermines a sense of meaning in life. That is no way to live. If life is to be lived fully, it cannot just be about existing and surviving.

I have been serving as a pastor for over twenty-five years. In the early years of my assignment someone once asked me, "What is the goal of life?" My response was laced with deep theological and philosophical insight. As a young pastor, I felt as though I was obligated to give an answer that displayed intellectual wrestling with this profound question. I can't remember what my answer was, but in my immaturity, I was more concerned with being impressive than impactful. After years of joy and pain, highs and lows, success and disappointment, I've come to discover that the goal of life is simple: to live. That's it. The goal of life is to live. That's our life assignment.

That never became clearer to me than on August 28, 2018. I had just landed back in New York at LaGuardia Airport, returning from Charleston, South Carolina, after preaching at the church of one of my closest friends. That morning my friend and his wife picked me up from the hotel and took me to the airport. I felt fine and there seemed to be nothing physically wrong with me. When I arrived at LaGuardia, I retrieved my car and made my way to the church for our executive team meeting.

As I was crossing the Robert F. Kennedy Bridge, the bridge that connects Queens to Manhattan, I suddenly lost the sight in my left eye. I instantly panicked. I had no idea what was going on. I literally began to feel my eye to make sure it was still there. I know that sounds crazy, but it all happened so fast that I was completely disoriented. I lost the sight in my left eye and everything seemed to be moving in slow motion.

When I crossed the bridge, I got off at the first exit, pulled my car over, and parked.

I called my wife and my assistant and told them I was experiencing a loss of sight in my left eye. They were both concerned. I told them that I would just sit in the car for about twenty minutes or so to see if my vision returned. If by then I still couldn't see, I would call 911. For years I had had issues with my left eye and I assumed that it was not that serious. Looking back on that moment, losing sight in my eye was an indication that something was wrong and I had no idea how serious it was.

The vision in my eye returned after about twenty minutes. I called my wife and assistant, informed them that I was fine, and said that I would meet them at the church. When I arrived at the church, I felt fine, the meeting was going well, and the mood in the room was light. Suddenly, I became extremely nauseated. The feeling was intense. I told my wife that I didn't feel well and asked her to walk with me to my office so that I could go to the bathroom. Before she could respond, I grabbed her by the hand and off we went. I have no idea why I asked her to come with me, but I'm pretty sure that, had I not, I would not be here today.

We got up from the conference room table and made our way to the door in order to go to my office. The last thing I remember was turning the knob on the conference room door. The next time I opened my eyes, I was in the emergency room of the hospital.

I was absolutely bewildered. I heard the doctor calling my name, but I thought I was dreaming. The taste of blood was in my mouth. The doctor called my name again. I felt fragments of my teeth in my mouth. My mind was racing. I saw my wife standing next to me with a look of concern on her face. She held my hand. The doctor asked me if I could hear him, and I nodded in affirmation. He said, "I need you to say 'yes.'" I tried to say yes, but I was having difficulty saying the word. Then it hit me: I had had a stroke.

I had a massive hemorrhagic stroke that was caused by a granuloma in my brain. Granulomas are areas of inflammation, like tumors. Apparently, as the granuloma in my brain got bigger, it put pressure on the blood vessels in the right temporal lobe until the vessels ruptured and caused a massive brain bleed. As the blood spread across my brain, it triggered seizures. The seizures are what caused me to lose consciousness, and while undergoing the seizure, the force from biting down broke teeth in the back of my mouth.

I struggled with my speech and my left arm and leg felt extremely stiff. I was in the hospital for about a week and even while in the hospital, the doctors were amazed by my recovery. I struggled with word recall, but my speech was almost like it was before the stroke. Although my arm and leg were still a little stiff, I could walk unassisted. It was a brutal ordeal, and it took me several months to fully recovery, but I was grateful to God that I survived.

In one of my follow-up visits with the neurologist, I remember feeling quite depressed. I had been experiencing something called auditory hallucinations, caused by the stroke. I was hearing things in my ears frequently. Most of the time it sounded like the loud rubbing of sandpaper. During the visit, the doctor could see I was not feeling good about the situation, and he started typing on his computer. I thought that was quite rude. He was just typing, appearing to not be listening to me at all.

He turned his screen around and showed me the images on the screen. They were MRIs of my brain immediately after the stroke. One side of my brain was bright in the MRI. The doctor told me that, on an MRI, blood appears as a bright light. He told me that most patients who experience the kind of stroke that I had either don't survive it or they are severely damaged by it. He then said, "Pastor, you survived the stroke, and you have no visible signs that you had a stroke." He went on to say, "If I showed my colleagues your MRIs and then introduced you to them, they would not believe that those images belonged to you. Pastor, you are a miracle." He was right. I was a miracle. I survived. Yes, I had a few neurological ticks, but I was alive. And with that, my depressive mood was gone, and I went home with a renewed attitude.

First, I was eternally grateful to God that I had survived the stroke. I have been through so many health issues in my life and it is clear that there is a powerful life-force within me. Ralph Waldo Emerson wrote, "Cultivate the habit of being grateful for every good thing that comes to you, and to give thanks continuously. And because all things have contributed to your advancement, you should include all things in your gratitude." Secondly, I thought about the fact that if I had died in August of 2018, the last thing I would have done before I died was to attend a meeting. A *meeting.* That would have been my last act on the planet—another meeting. Therefore, I established new criteria to help me make certain decisions moving forward. The criteria I established for decision-making does not work for all things, but it sure changed my perspective. Here it is: The only way I can say yes to certain endeavors is if I'm fine with it potentially being the last thing I may ever do. Life is short and we never know what the next moment may bring, but I want to make decisions that I can feel good dying with. It may sound morbid, but it changes the things you say yes to. And first and foremost, I have to be able to say yes *to* me and *for* me. My stroke taught me that.

Life is truly a journey filled with episodes that can cause spontaneous eruptions of joy or ignite emotions that fan the flames of misery. This is the nature of the journey: mountaintop moments that we wish would never end and valley visitations that feel like eternal anguish.

It is the ebb and flow of life, the wonder and the riddles, the beauty and blight that perplex us. In our secret and sacred longings, we yearn for the sun to never stop shining and wish we had the power to forbid the oncoming dark. But that would mean a half-lived life. The journey is perplexing and at times confounding, but it still has the capacity to yield beautiful fruit.

Do not seek to avoid the dark times that will come, but all of life, the good and the bad, has the potential to birth possibilities.

In the Old Testament, Genesis begins with the story of creation. The story indicates that the world was void and without form, and darkness was upon the face of the deep. It was out of that darkness that God began to move and create. Imagine that for a moment and, as one of my mentors would say, let that thought marinate in your spirit.

Genesis suggests that darkness was the context out of which creation began. Darkness was not the enemy. Like the womb that bears the gift until the day of delivery, darkness was that out of which new life was birthed. The idea that God creates in the dark and out of the darkness gives us a new way of appropriating the dark times that may come along in life's mystifying journey. Instead of avoiding the dark times, and risk living a half-lived life, maybe one of the main tasks along the journey is to learn to embrace the dark times.

I am not suggesting that one go looking for dark moments or try to create them, but I am suggesting that in avoiding the darkness, in avoiding challenging times, an opportunity for growth and new life may be missed. At times along my journey, I wanted blissful moments to never end. I did not want the joy I felt in those interludes to come to an end. I found myself holding on to moments that became exhausted of true value. I wanted so badly to linger in the ecstasy of bright moments that had already passed that I missed the opportunities that may have been waiting in the next episode of my journey. The humbling reality is that the next episode may be shaped by the dark times that one seeks to avoid, but that same darkness can also bring forth new life.

Do not simply retreat and surrender in the face of the challenging times that will come along in your journey. Resolve in your spirit that when the unavoidable and painful realities of living manifest themselves in your life, that you will view those moments as an opportunity to create in the dark.

External obstacles and barriers make living a quite difficult endeavor. People will try to make life difficult for others because their own lives are shaped by misery. Tragic life circumstances and situations that are beyond our control can rob life of its joy. External obstacles and barriers are real, but the most dangerous obstacles to living are internal.

The negative attitudes and feelings we have about ourselves are the greatest hindrances to living. When we feel unworthy of joy or beauty or peace, then living is marginalized and angst and depression can shape our days. Ironically, in an attempt to bypass feelings of unworthiness, we often engage in attention-seeking activities, but when does that stop? The more attention you seek and receive, the more you need it, and the more you need it, the more you lose yourself trying to attain it. The real you dies. The manufactured you lives.

Life is fragile and fleeting. Death is inevitable, but living is optional. I want the real you to live, not the you that is an assembly of counterfeit parts.

Sometimes our ability to live is determined by our willingness to confront ourselves and not be afraid of what we discover in the confrontation. But what we discover will not destroy us, especially if we enter the journey of self-discovery knowing that we are God's provision for a time hungry for authenticity. We are God's Joy. We are Agabus. We are enough. And nothing we discover about ourselves can ever change that.

Dare to Live

If you know how quickly people forget the dead, you'll stop living to impress people.

—Christopher Walken

Live life to the fullest. Tomorrow may never be.

—Shah Rukh Khan

For every death, there is a new birth, and I have come to realize that death and dying are part of the cycle of life. By no means does this ease the sting that one feels when death shows up without warning, but we are reminded that there can be no life without death.

Several years ago, someone very close to me suddenly and unexpectedly passed away. She was a woman who helped raise me. She would often tell people that she was my second mother, but she was my god sister. She had an indelible impact on my life. She was the one who taught me the alphabet and how to write in cursive. She was one of my greatest cheerleaders, and she consistently encouraged me not to be afraid to be myself.

When I received word of her passing, I was devastated. The dam had burst and the flow of tears did not recede. I was blindsided by grief, and the instant heaviness I felt almost made my spirit buckle. In my younger days, I did not have the emotional resources to handle the moments when death would raise its head and make an uninvited appearance. As a child, I did not understand the permanence of physical disconnection that accompanied death. In those days, before my faith in God was born, I was offended by the arrival of death—angry at the intruder. Now, my walk with God has been a source of tremendous strength, and I no longer see death as an interloper because we are all future memories.

A few days before my god sister died, she called me and told me how proud she was of me and how much she loved me. I can still hear her encouraging words and feel the warmth of her spirit. I will miss her. I will miss her illuminating smile and her infectious laugh. The last thing she told me was to never stop chasing my dreams. As I reflect on her last words to me, I am aware that it takes tremendous bravery and courage to pursue dreams, especially when those dreams are about being who you've never been, going where you've never gone, and doing what you've never done. But I am also aware that fear is the greatest enemy we have when it comes to pursuing our dreams.

It is amazing how at times our greatest dreams have a way of colliding with our greatest fears. We never really plan for the collision because there is a part of us that wants to believe that the nobility of our dreams can transcend the shadows of our character. We hope against hope that the secretly harbored thoughts that are connected to our feelings of inadequacy will never escape the emotional labyrinth we construct to protect us from ourselves.

We construct these illusory protections because it is too difficult to accept that there is something within us—something unsettling—that seeks to sabotage the beautiful dreams that were conceived in the peaceful places of the soul. Our fears are the unavoidable saboteurs that we long to assassinate, only to discover that the attempt to destroy fears that have not been confronted is the equivalent of emotional suicide.

Confronting the fears that dwell deep within us is difficult work. The work is so difficult that many of us would rather engage in self-deception, and either act like the fears are fabricated—and thereby easily dismissed—or create a false facade of strength and behave as though the fears have no real impact. Neither approach contributes to growth.

I have come to realize that the fears we have tried so hard to ignore have a way of manifesting themselves at the most inopportune times. One of those inopportune times is when we are pursuing our dreams. Have you ever found yourself in hot pursuit of your dreams only to have your pursuit derailed by your fears? Have you ever given up on the goals you have set for yourself because you could not bypass the mountain of fear that stood in the way?

I have been there before, and it is never a pleasant experience. There is something spiritually and emotionally incapacitating that takes place when the fears we have tried to avoid for so long rear their ugly heads just when we are about to actualize grand visions for our lives. I believe this happens because becoming who and what we desire to be cannot be fully achieved without being honest with ourselves, and being honest with ourselves means being honest about what we fear.

If we remain dishonest, we simply set ourselves up for failure, because true transformation cannot take place when self-deception is a coping mechanism to deal with fear. The aspirations we hold close to our hearts will not become real unless we are willing to face our fears. Again, I am quite cognizant of the difficulty involved when it comes to confronting fears, but I also know of the joy waiting on the other side of the confrontation. Just imagine getting to know the *you* who existed before you let your fears reconstruct your identity. Just imagine how much lighter your days will be when you no longer have to carry the weight of self-deception. But in order to do that, you must be willing to confront fears. And one of the fears that may be behind much of the narcissistic behavior that is so prevalent today is the fear of being irrelevant.

The fear of being irrelevant can be suffocating. The idea of living a purposeless life is terrifying, but also motivates us to participate in projects that we believe will give us longevity beyond our last breath. Many have lost themselves in root-less pursuits with the hope that somehow a list and legacy of accomplishments will give their lives meaning because we do not want to be viewed as unnecessary.

But motivated by fear, some engage in paradoxical behavior. Paradoxical because in our desire to be relevant, we seek validation from external sources and, in that pursuit, it is possible to lose one's self in a haze of conformity. In other words, the quest for relevance can lead to conforming to the expectations of people who have no investment in your future. When this is done, one's distinctiveness is lost and being irrelevant becomes a possibility.

Living life between your greatest hopes and the expecta-tions of others can be a recipe for misery. Your spirit becomes weary from the tug-of-war between your longed-for aspira-tions and the limited imagination of those who want you to be content with mediocrity. When this fatigue sets in, the joy that ignited life-giving dreams is lost because you become fearful of letting others down. The inner voice that pushes you to be your better self is drowned out by the many voices that tell you to live cautiously because the safe life is free of failure.

And those who encourage the safe life offer a prescription for safety that has been developed from their own fears. There is nothing worse than taking advice from people who have never sought to mount wings of possibility and soar to unimaginable heights. Living a life of relevance is not just about existing. You must dare to live. There will always be people who will try to hold you captive in their fears because they lack the courage to engage with life fully. Do not let those people have the last word over your life. Do not let those people put a stranglehold on your destiny.

Choosing to live can be risky business, but merely existing is the death that arrives before dying. Erwin McManus, the spiritual leader of Mosaic Church in Los Angeles, once wrote, "What a tragedy to breathe your last breath and to discover that your life was not only unfinished but perhaps never really even began." Therefore, dare to live.

As I write this, the chill of winter has descended upon us and a new year has begun. For those who have been romanced by regret, barren trees and early darkness signal a season of discontent. We look back on the year that has passed and mourn what could have been in the warmer, light-filled days. All of us have been tempted to wallow in regret. We look back over the previous year and remember how it started with so much hope and promise, only to feel like the seasons were wasted on dreams that never landed in the realm of reality.

Regret is a dangerous foe. It can paralyze possibilities and cause depression. There have been times in my life when it felt like I could not break free from the clutches of regret and, in those anxious moments, I found myself constantly lamenting what was lost—lost time, lost opportunity, lost relationships, lost people, lost days. I discovered that my problem was that I was living in my "yesterday." I was so consumed by the time that had already passed that I was not living in my present.

Days were passing me by because I was grieving over days that were already dead. That was not living. That was dying a slow death.

Albert Einstein once said, "Learn from yesterday, live for today, hope for tomorrow." Too many of us find ourselves dying because we are living in yesterday and the yesterday we are living in is filled with tainted memories that can be brutal. It is easy to get lost in yesterday's sorrow, but the key to rebelling against regret is remembering that when yesterday gives you a hundred reasons to cry, today can give you a thousand reasons to smile. There is no need to perform emotional CPR on a dead past. Learn from the past, but live for today.

One of my favorite movies is *The Shawshank Redemption*. Andy Dufresne, the main character, spent 19 years in prison for a murder he did not commit. During those 19 years, Andy was digging a tunnel to escape. The day before Andy was to make his great escape, he told Red, his best friend in prison, that in life "you either get busy living or get busy dying." Andy believed that his escape from prison was necessary if he was going to live.

Andy's words may resonate with you. You've been reading this book and realized that you have been living in a prison fashioned by your own hands. You have had accomplices in the construction of the prison that has held you captive and now you are regretting all of it. You regret letting others determine the parameters of your life. Here is my word to you: Get busy living or get busy dying. Living in regret over what was is death business, but learning to live for today is the greatest investment you can make

Ernest Hemingway once wrote: "Today is only one day in all the days that will ever be. But what will happen in all the other days that ever come can depend on what you do today." Today, I dare you to make every breath count. I dare you to reject agendas that have been heaped upon you by people who do not want the best for you. I dare you to assault your deepest fears with your greatest dreams. Get busy living!

Into the Silence

When you begin to become aware of who God designed you to be you start shedding the energies that are not in alignment with the frequency of your life.

—Negal de la Casa

Numerous are the tentacles of sexual assault. The only thing that compares to the reach of its brutality is the introspection it births which, escorted by pain, can be dislodging and destructive. This may be why Michaela Coel's *I May Destroy You* resonated with so many—the tentacles are far reaching and the pain expressed by Arabella, the series's main character, is palpable. Arabella's quest to make sense of her life before and after her sexual assault speaks to many who have had to gather the fragments left after the intrusion of brokenness. Thus, it came as no surprise to me when I found out that Coel had won an Emmy award for the series and made history at the same time.

In 2021, Coel became the first black woman to win an Emmy for Outstanding Writing for a Limited or Anthology Series or Movie. She not only wrote the series, but she starred in and directed it as well. It was an incredible accomplishment. She dedicated her award to survivors of sexual assault not because it was the politically correct thing to do, but because it was the right thing to do.

Coel stood in solidarity with fellow survivors. Her art was the overflow of her reality. *I May Destroy You* was based on her story of sexual assault. Her transparency, vulnerability, and authenticity was salvific for many who have suffered in silence as they navigated the rugged emotional and psychological terrain of sexual assault's aftermath. Coel receiving the award was profound on many levels.

When she received the award, Coel was visibly emotional—and expectedly so. Her acceptance speech was profound and beautiful and there was a part of her speech that resonated with me as I was writing this book. She said, "Visibility these days seems to somehow equate with success. Do not be afraid to disappear from it, from us for a while, and see what comes to you in the silence." Her words struck a chord with me, especially since I was working on a book about the under-side of the desire to be visible, to be seen, to be validated. It was as if she were giving marching orders to those whose souls are knowingly or unknowingly weary from equating visibility with success. Her directive seemed clear: disappear into the silence.

The world is a noisy place, filled with distracting sounds—deafening, unpleasant sounds, seemingly committed to disturbance and disruption. Some of the loudest, most distracting noises that we are bombarded with, almost every day, are the reckless reverberations that tell us that we are not "enough." Enormous amounts of money are invested in marketing schemes that prey on personal feelings of inadequacy that abound in the world. Obscene amounts of money are being made off low self-esteem and the victims of these schemes are left emotionally depleted. What can be done to combat the noise? What can be done to drown out the depleting noise? We must learn to disappear into the silence and discover our own sound. For that discovery is the key to living and life.

Disappearing for a time will not be easy because whether we like to admit it or not, many of us are addicted to the noise and crave its company. In that regard, retreating into the silence is terrifying and we do not always want to discover our own sound or honor our own uniqueness. Tragically, it is much easier to accept what you have been told about who you are than to lean into the mystery of your own humanity. I know the journey for self-discovery can be painful, but pain can be a necessary midwife whose value is not always seen until some semblance of wholeness is achieved. And just as the pain of childbirth is the precursor to the first unassisted breath of a newborn, so too our pain can have a way of giving birth to breath and life.

Disappearing for a time does not mean falling completely off the grid, although at times retreating from the grind of life is necessary for sustaining your sanity. Disappearing for a time means retreating into anonymity and rebelling against the idea that visibility is synonymous with success. Discover the silent spaces and places within you. Replace the hunger for attention with an insatiable hunger for healing and restoration. Do not allow the noise of the world to silence your rareness. There is no one like you, and so refuse to accept the shards leftover from a life partially lived. Your authenticity is your superpower. Embrace the silence so you can hear the whispers of your soul.

So, go. Disappear into the silence for a time. Unplug. Disconnect. It will not be easy, but it is necessary if you are going to breathe free and live free. Again, it will not be easy, and you will encounter much on your journey but inside each breath, inside each suffering, inside each tear, inside each smile, inside each hurt, inside each tragedy, inside each joy, wisdom is waiting, longing to make you wiser and stronger. So, go. Disappear into the silence for a time. Find your way back to you. Agabus will be with you. You will be with you. You are all you need. You are the joy needed for the journey. Your strength will find a resting place inhabited by your resilience, and your soul will thank you for your heart's generosity.

Acknowledgments

No one accomplishes anything of significance on their own, and this book is no different. There are many who have served as companions along the journey of writing this book. I am deeply indebted to my wife, who I met at a time when the numerous facades I created were unraveling and who accepted me and loved me when all I could see was my damage and my wounds. For that I am grateful. I would like to also express gratitude to my son and my daughter, Tre and Jasmyn, whose love for me is a constant reminder that life is bigger than me. My mother and my brother's constant belief in me made the difficult days fade away.

I learned a long time ago that friendship is essential to the soul. I want to thank Maurice Wallace, A. Byron Coleman, Tory Liferidge, Darron Johnson, Laverne King, and my assistant, Sharon Chancie. They each heard or read different parts of this book. Their friendship, honesty, and graciousness were sources of support and encouragement.

I could not have taken the time necessary to complete this book were it not for the leadership and support of the Executive Team, Staff, Deacons, Trustees and Disciples of the First Corinthian Baptist Church of Harlem, New York. I am humbled to be a part of such an amazing church. And a special thank you to Adrienne Ingrum and all at Broadleaf who believed in this book.

Finally, I want to thank my grandfather, the late Edwin St. Clair Walrond, whose love encouraged me to find my way back to me.